The Rosedata Stone

Achieving a
Common Business Language
using the
Business Terms Model

Steve Hoberman

Technics Publications

Published by:

2 Lindsley Road, Basking Ridge, NJ 07920 USA
https://www.TechnicsPub.com

Edited by Riaz Howey
Cover design by Lorena Molinari

First Printing 2020
Copyright © 2020 by Steve Hoberman

ISBN, print ed.	9781634627733
ISBN, Kindle ed.	9781634627740
ISBN, ePub ed.	9781634627757
ISBN, PDF ed.	9781634627764

Library of Congress Control Number: 2020931193

To Jenn.

Contents

Introduction

Are you familiar with the Rosetta Stone? This 2000-year-old slab contains the same message in multiple scripts, permitting modern scholars who were able to read Ancient Greek to decipher Egyptian hieroglyphs.

Similar to how the Rosetta Stone provided a communication tool across languages, the *Rosedata Stone* provides a communication tool across business languages. The Rosedata Stone, called the *Business Terms Model* (BTM) or the *Conceptual Data Model*, displays a Common Business Language of terms for a particular business initiative.

With more and more data being created and used, combined with intense competition, strict regulations, and rapid-spread social media, the financial, liability, and credibility stakes have never been higher and therefore the need for a Common Business Language has never been greater. Appreciate the power of the BTM and apply the steps to build a BTM over the book's five chapters:

1. **Challenges**. Explore how a Common Business Language is more important than ever with technologies like the Cloud and NoSQL, and Regulations such as the GDPR.

2. **Needs**. Identify scope and plan precise, minimal visuals that will capture the Common Business Language.

3. **Solution**. Meet the BTM and its components, along with the variations of relational and dimensional BTMs. Experience how several data modeling tools display the BTM, including CaseTalk, ER/Studio, erwin DM, and Hackolade.

4. **Construction**. Build operational (relational) and analytics (dimensional) BTMs for a bakery chain.

5. **Practice**. Reinforce BTM concepts and build BTMs for two of your own initiatives.

This book is written for both business and information technology professionals, with an emphasis on project managers, data governance professionals, and business analysts. Although some of this material might be a review for data architects and data modelers, these data professionals can use the knowledge gained from this book to broaden, challenge, or refine their perspectives.

There are two styles used throughout this book. We use italics when we are discussing a technical or business name. For example, Bob calls it *customer* and Jane calls it *consumer*. We use bold when we are discussing terms. For example, a **Customer** may place many **Orders**.

Are you ready? Let's get started!

CHAPTER 1

Challenges

Imagine you are the Chief Information Officer for the bakery chain Chips Inc. Not only do you receive a salary and health benefits, but you also can eat as many pastries as you like for free from any of the 30 bakeries that Chips Inc. owns and operates. Now that is a great job perk!

Due to the independent culture of Chips Inc.—combined with how Chips Inc. grew by buying a bakery at a time—each bakery has its own way of operating. Each bakery uses its own systems such as Quicken, Excel, and sometimes even pencil and paper, to assist with ordering supplies, baking pastries, managing sales, and handling payroll.

With costs for raw materials such as sugar on the rise, and increased competition from other bakeries and high-end supermarkets, Chips Inc.'s executives are looking for ways to save money and therefore increase profits. One way is the potential savings in centralizing pastry purchasing followed by a centralized payroll. Centralizing business processes such as purchasing should not only save money, but also allow for more consistent reporting across the organization, identifying additional ways to save money and uncovering new business opportunities.

In addition, Chips Inc. would like to franchise their brand, recipes, and processes to other bakeries. Prior to approaching bakeries on franchising opportunities, Chips Inc. needs to follow more consistent practices across their 30 stores. Once consistent practices are in place, they can be applied to the franchisee bakeries.

The executive team is convinced—mostly due to a one-hour sales pitch presentation from a large software consulting organization—that centralizing business processes will take minimal effort. The presenter touted his software solution as a seamless way to integrate all Chips Inc. processes. "It's as easy as baking a cookie," this software consultant said as the executives nodded their heads in hypnotic agreement. You, however, are not as optimistic. And it's not just because you find baking a challenge. You wonder how a software solution can magically solve a very complex business problem.

After lunch you stroll down the road to Chips Inc.'s flagship bakery to treat yourself to a free chocolate chip cookie. After showing the store employee your Chips Inc. badge and receiving your free cookie, you browse the tantalizing cakes, cupcakes, and cookies.

As an attempt to convince yourself of the similarity across bakeries, you decide to take a bus ride to another Chips Inc. bakery on the other side of town within an upscale neighborhood. Since this bakery caters to a higher-end clientele, what was called a *cookie* at the last bakery is called a *biscuit* in this bakery. This bakery has an extensive pie selection yet no cakes. They also sell parfaits, smoothies, and artisan breads which the first bakery did not carry.

As you munch on a free chocolate chip *biscuit* (which tastes strikingly similar to a chocolate chip *cookie*), questions start brewing:

- How do cookies and biscuits differ?
- How do pies and cakes differ?
- Are artisan breads, smoothies, and parfaits within the scope of the pastry purchasing initiative?

Successfully purchasing ingredients for our bakeries requires a common set of terms. Asking the first bakery how much sugar they order for *biscuits* and the second bakery how much sugar they order for *cookies* would most likely cause confusion as the first bakery calls them *cookies* and the second *biscuits*. In addition, a third bakery sells dog *biscuits* which have different ingredients and therefore different purchasing requirements than the *biscuits* from the second bakery.

Note that it is ok for the first bakery to keep calling them *cookies* and for the second bakery to keep calling them *biscuits*, if they are recognized by the corporate purchaser to be the same thing. This will require a common term that disambiguates all of the variations. Similar to the Rosetta Stone translating between ancient scripts, the Rosedata Stone translates between terms from different departments or locations. For example, Bakery A calls it *cookie*, Bakery B calls it *biscuit*, other bakeries have their own terms, and the corporate purchaser calls it *cookie*. The corporate purchaser would be the common term across the bakeries.

The corporate purchaser's **Cookie** is the common term and the mapping on the facing page provides the purchaser with a translation to each of the localized terms. Determining a centralized order for sugar requires the purchaser to use the term **Biscuit** when communicating with Store B and **Sweet Cake** with Store C.

Rosedata Stone Mapping

```
                    ┌──────────────┐
                    │  Store A:    │
                    │  Cookie      │
                    └──────────────┘
                           ↕
┌──────────┐        ┌──────────────┐        ┌──────────┐
│ Store E: │        │  Corporate   │        │ Store B: │
│ Drop     │ ◄────► │  Purchaser:  │ ◄────► │ Biscuit  │
└──────────┘        │  Cookie      │        └──────────┘
                    └──────────────┘
                       ↙        ↘
            ┌──────────┐        ┌──────────┐
            │ Store D: │        │ Store C: │
            │ Crisp    │        │ Sweet    │
            └──────────┘        │ Cake     │
                                └──────────┘
```

This type of mapping is very useful for showing a common term and its translation to the multi-language reality of our current environment.

Chips Inc. executives, for example, believes centralizing purchasing will be easy without realizing that each bakery speaks their own unique language. Or maybe management acknowledges the lack of a Common Business Language but assumes a software solution will magically solve the problems. It does not matter, though, if the two bakeries you visited that day both use the same system such as

Microsoft Excel, if one bakery calls it *cookie* and the other *biscuit*, there are going to be challenges in centralizing purchasing.

We will see in Chapter 4 that a mapping diagram such as the one above, combined with powerful visuals such as the one below, will improve communication within your initiatives and therefore lead to more successful software solutions and a stronger rapport between business and information technology professionals.

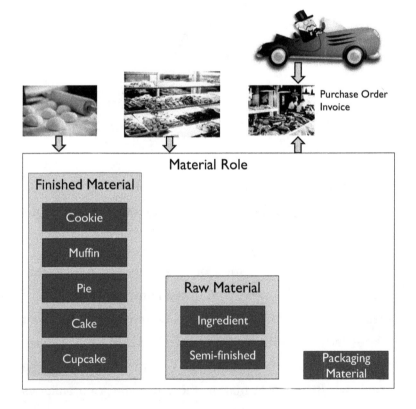

Although we will use the Chips Inc. bakery business throughout the book, the challenges can easily be projected to your organization. Have you had similar experiences where it seems someone you are working with is using Ancient Greek and someone else Hieroglyphics?

I've had many experiences where people who need to speak a Common Business Language are not using the same set of terms consistently. For example, I recently facilitated a discussion between a senior business analyst and senior manager at a large insurance company.

The senior manager expressed his frustration on how a business analyst was slowing down the development of his business analytics application. "The team was meeting with the product owner and business users to get the user stories on insurance quotes complete for our upcoming analytics application on quotes, when a business analyst asked the question, *What is a quote?* and the rest of the meeting was wasted on trying to answer this question. Why couldn't we just focus on getting the requirements for Quote Analytics, which is what we were in that meeting to do? We are supposed to be Agile!"

If there was a lengthy discussion trying to clarify the meaning of a quote, there is a very good chance this billion dollar insurance company does not have a good understanding of a *quote*. It is possible that all business users agree that a quote is an estimate for a policy premium, but disagree at what point an estimate becomes a quote. For example, does an estimate have to be based on a certain percentage of facts before it can be considered a quote?

How well will Quote Analytics meet the user requirements if the users are not clear as to what a *quote* is? Imagine needing to know the answer to this question:

How many life insurance quotes were written last quarter in the northeast?

Without a common understanding of *quote*, it is possible for one user to answer this question based on their definition of *quote*, and someone else to answer based on their different definition of *quote*. One of these users (or possibly both) will most likely get the wrong answer.

I've worked with a university whose employees could not come to agreement on what a *student* meant, a manufacturing company whose sales and accounting departments differed on the meaning of *return on total assets*, a financial company whose analysts battled relentlessly over the meaning of a *trade*—it's all the same challenge we need to overcome, isn't it?

It's about working towards a Common Business Language.

A Common Business Language is a prerequisite for success in any initiative. We can capture and communicate the terms underlying business processes and requirements, enabling people with different backgrounds and roles to understand and communicate with each other.

In a recent study, 89% of senior managers surveyed from over 1,000 organizations faced challenges in how they manage data.[1] I am convinced after decades of working with data in countries around the globe, and in almost every industry, that the root cause of these challenges in managing data is a lack of speaking a Common Business Language.

Let's face the hurdles of technology, expectations, and ambiguity that must be overcome to arrive at a Common Business Language. The first step to solve a challenge is to fully understand it, and we are ready to do just that.

Technology

Travel back with me to the year 1978.

The New York Yankees win the World Series, Montreal takes the Stanley Cup, Borg is the Wimbledon champion, and Argentina wins the World Cup. *Annie*

---

[1] 2019 Experian Global Data Management Research Report, https://bit.ly/2RHmeJp.

Hall wins the Oscar for Best Picture, *You Light Up My Life* wins the Oscar for best song, and the record of the year is *Hotel California* by The Eagles. We can reminisce on fashion (and yes, I did own a pair of bell bottoms) and politics (Peanuts, anybody?), but instead, let's look at the world of technology in 1978.

1978 was a monumental year for technology. Sony introduced the world's first portable stereo, the Sony Walkman. Also in 1978, Illinois Bell Company introduced the first cellular mobile phone system. Do you remember those "portable" large shoulder-bag mobile phones first came in? This same year, the first computer bulletin board system (BBS) was created. (I remember buying a used refrigerator off a BBS.) Also monumental this year, Space Invaders made its debut and the craze for video games began.

In addition to the start of the age for portable music, cell phones, online commerce, and video games, 1978 was also a banner year for data management. The relational model had a big win over the hierarchical and network models: Oracle Version 1 was announced in 1978, written in assembly language and running on a whopping 128K of memory. And also in 1978, William Kent wrote *Data and Reality*.[2]

---

[2] *Data and Reality: A Timeless Perspective on Perceiving and Managing Information in Our Imprecise World*, 3rd ed., William Kent, Technics Publications, 2012.

This excerpt from the preface I wrote to the 3rd edition of William Kent's classic, *Data and Reality,* paints a picture of the available technology when the 1st edition of *Data and Reality* was published in 1978.

Data and Reality contains many examples illustrating poor communication across departments and business areas. Kent iterates how important it is to have in place a common understanding of terms before building or buying software solutions.

We can do more on our watches today than the most powerful computers in 1978, yet with all of our amazing technologies, we still have not solved the communication issues Kent raised in 1978!

Data and Reality contains an entire chapter on understanding a "book", as an example of making us aware of how ambiguous even simple terms can be. Here is one of my favorite statements from this chapter:

> So, once again, if we are going to have a database about books, before we can know what one representative stands for, we had better have a consensus among all users as to what "one book" is. [3]

---

[3] *Data and Reality: A Timeless Perspective on Perceiving and Managing Information in Our Imprecise World,* 3rd ed., William Kent, Technics Publications, 2012.

Summarizing this quote, William Kent is saying that before we build an application, know what the terms mean. Before we build a cloud-based policy application for an insurance company, know what a **Policy** is. Before we build a NoSQL application for a publishing company, know what a **Book** is. Before we implement a Customer Relationship Management (CRM) solution for a manufacturing company, know what a **Customer** is. This advice might sound obvious—but is it followed?

Technologies create a false perception that others are responsible for understanding our data. The cloud means a hosting company will store our data and therefore they must understand our data. NoSQL means a database vendor will structure our data and therefore they must understand our data. Packages means a vendor will provide software to process our data and therefore they must understand our data.

Cloud

The cloud means a hosting company will store and protect our data. The cloud can also increase uncertainty (cloudiness?) of what data is stored where, making it more difficult to understand our data and therefore business terms, and ultimately more challenging to achieve a Common Business Language. If some of our product information is stored in the cloud, it could make understanding product more challenging—what do we call that subset of product data stored in the cloud and that which we store inhouse?

Organizations who assume hosting companies will take responsibility for understanding their data will not be working in the cloud anymore, but in a tornado funnel.

NoSQL

Since the 1970s, most of our organizations' data has been stored in Relational Database Management Systems, the formal term for relational databases. A relational database stores data in sets. Just like you can have a set for cats and a set for dogs, a set for even numbers and a set for odd numbers, a set for cars and a set for bicycles, you can have a set for **Customer** data, a set for **Product** data, and a set for **Employee** data.

The process of organizing data into sets to store in a relational database is called *normalization.* Normalizing data uncovers the meaning and connections within the data, providing us with a strong understanding of the overarching terms in the process. For example, once customer data has been normalized, we will better understand **Customer.**

NoSQL means data can be stored in an unorganized text format instead of an organized set format. You can store data using NoSQL almost as easily as storing text in a Microsoft Word document. Without the forced rigor to organize data into sets however, many project teams implement NoSQL applications with little knowledge of what terms mean. Even with the latest technology, we are still doing what William Kent said not to do back in 1978—building a database about books before really knowing what a book is.

Packages

Vendor packages such as those offered by SAP, Oracle, and Microsoft can be huge "black boxes" that excel at getting data in and out (storing and analyzing data) but hide how data is actually organized. Employees often lack knowledge of the internal structures—and therefore lack knowledge of what the terms being stored and analyzed really mean.

I spent four years of my career in the bowels of SAP in an area called *Classifications*. This area of SAP allowed organizations to run reports at higher levels than a particular product, such as a report run against the brand classification or against the product size classification. Before I joined this team, people knew how to load data from external systems into Classifications and how to extract data from Classifications, but few understood the terms within Classifications until we created a BTM containing **Class, Characteristic, Characteristic Value, Object,** and other important terms within this area.

Having a common language around terms such as **Class** and **Characteristic** (which were often incorrectly used interchangeably), allowed our department to discuss enhancements to this area and know we were speaking the same language.

Organizations frequently select vendor packages to solve business process issues, yet introducing a new application usually raises term issues. For example, an organization might want to improve their logistics process through a vendor package. However, the vendor package uses different names than the organization, or the same names but different meanings, for even basic terms like **Customer** or **Product.** If you ask someone within logistics what a **Product** means, they will need to clarify, "Do you mean our definition or the vendor's?"

In addition, most packages are built generically to fit many different organizations. Referring back to Classifications for example, **Object** encompasses customer, vendor, and product. Not only do we still need to understand **Customer, Vendor,** and **Product,** we now have one more term to learn. What's an **Object?**

Ambiguity

> We are dealing with a natural ambiguity of words,
> which we, as human beings, resolve in a largely
> automatic and unconscious way, because we understand
> the context in which the words are being used. When a
> data file exists to serve just one application, there is, in
> effect, just one context, and users implicitly understand
> that context; they automatically resolve ambiguities by
> interpreting words as appropriate for that context. But
> when files get integrated into a database serving
> multiple applications, that ambiguity-resolving
> mechanism is lost. The assumptions appropriate to the
> context of one application may not fit the contexts of
> other applications:[4]

This passage from the 1978 classic, *Data and Reality*, nicely
captures the challenge that our spoken and written
communication is naturally ambiguous. We keep the
conversation interesting by not repeating the same words
again and again, so it is common to use similar words
instead. Imagine this conversation by the coffee machine at
a university:

---

[4] *Data and Reality: A Timeless Perspective on Perceiving and Managing Information in Our Imprecise World*, 3rd ed., William Kent, Technics Publications, 2012.

Bob: How's your course going?

Mary: Going well. But my students are complaining about too much homework. They tell me they have many other classes.

Bob: The attendees in my advanced session say the same thing.

Mary: I wouldn't expect that from graduates. Anyway, how many other offerings are you teaching this semester?

Bob: I'm teaching five offerings this term and one is an evening not-for-credit class.

We can let this conversation continue for a few pages, but do you see the ambiguity caused by this simple dialog?

- What is the difference between **Course**, **Class**, **Offering**, and **Session**?
- Are **Semester** and **Term** the same?
- Are **Student** and **Attendee** the same?

Expectations

Since the 1970s, the goal of information management is to "get the *right* information to the *right* people at the *right* time." Every programming language, every database, every reporting tool—it should all bring us closer to this goal.

Today demands on our organizations are increasing at such a rapid rate that "getting the right information to the right people at the right time" is a constantly moving target. Similar to Tantalus who is forever hungry in Hades despite being almost within reach of a fruit tree, just when we think we have satisfied the necessary requirements, new and more demanding requirements appear hungry for even more information for the right people at the right time. The "right information" is not just customer sales from the northeast, but global sales. The "right people" is not just for the head of sales, but for all salespeople worldwide. The "right time" is not just last quarter's sales but last second's sales.

Agility

The business expects more powerful applications in shorter and shorter timeframes. Agile to the rescue. Agile is all about rapid application development. We can deliver applications quickly, but it takes time to discuss the meanings of terms and especially to come to agreement. Lengthy discussions on defining terms often appear counter to the spirit of Agile. Recall that insurance company manager who considered the discussions on the meaning of *quote* as wasted time.

In addition, often due to pressures to speed up development, the scope of initiatives becomes sharply reduced, and therefore there is rarely an opportunity to view important business terms at a broad enough scope to achieve a Common Business Language. On many Agile projects, the most we hope for is a common language within the very narrow scope of the iterative development cycle, such as in a Sprint.

Analytics

The business questions asked today are broader and require a faster answer than those asked only a few years ago. A question such as "Did this order get there on time?" is a much easier question to answer than "How many orders across all lines of business for this particular customer were received this quarter, and how does this compare with last year same quarter?"

We cannot answer these questions however unless there is agreement on the meaning of **Order**, **Customer**, and **Quarter**.

We are so conditioned to using search engines and seeing near-instant results from across the world, that we expect the same from our internal systems. A user would like to run a sales report for a particular customer, and see all sales for that customer, even though the sales data might exist in ten different applications that don't interface with each other. In addition, sales might have different names in different systems, and that customer might have different names in different systems. It is not as easy as retrieving text in a Google search.

Regulations

Our organizations are expected to follow regulations such as the General Data Protection Regulation (GDPR) Act in Europe, the Markets in Financial Instruments Directive (MiFID) and the Cybersecurity Law of the People's Republic of China (CSL), and in California with the California Consumer Privacy Act.

All of these regulations come down to knowing what data is stored, where it is stored, and how it was collected. We cannot have intelligent conversations to determine the what, where, and how of data unless we understand the overarching terms.

Takeaways

- Software solutions can help the business solve business problems but cannot solve the business problems without business involvement.

- It is ok for departments to continue using different names for the same term, as long as there is a translation between them to a common term.

- Often management does not want to invest time in creating a Common Business Language because they believe that a Common Business Language already exists somewhere, or that technology will solve the problem.

- Technologies create a false perception that others are responsible for understanding our data. The cloud means a hosting company will store our data and therefore they must understand our data. NoSQL means a database vendor will structure our data and therefore they must understand our data. Packages means a vendor will provide software to process our data and therefore they must understand our data.

- Our spoken and written communication is naturally ambiguous, and therefore we cannot deliver sophisticated analytics applications quickly and adhere to all government regulations without a Common Business Language.

CHAPTER 2

Needs

"I know this is hard Ms. Egg, but point to the person who beat you."

Recall from the prior chapter how even a simple term like **Cookie**, can have multiple names and meanings across bakeries.

Rosedata Stone Mapping

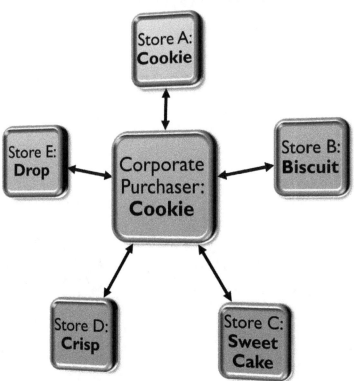

After identifying the challenges of technology, ambiguity, and expectation covered in Chapter 1, we need to understand each bakery's perspective. Ideally, employees at each of the bakeries along with corporate need to agree on a common term and definition. Practically, we will often end up with a diagram such as the one above that can maintain a mapping to the different perspectives.

It is not easy to complete mappings such as the one above, and even more challenging to agree on a Common Business Language.

Understanding the scope of our initiative ensures the Common Business Language we create provides value for the initiative and for the organization, and that the Common Business Language can be delivered in a reasonable time and does not overwhelm. Once we've confirmed scope, we need to transform the ambiguity in our verbal and sometimes written communication into a precise language. Precision does not mean detailed, such as showing database fields—we need to keep our language simple. In addition, following the maxim "a picture is worth a thousand words", we need visuals to communicate this precise and simple language for the initiative. These four needs of scope, precision, simplicity, and visuals are the subject of this chapter.

Scope

Does an organization need to have a Common Business Language across its entire enterprise?

Eventually, yes, it would provide substantial value.

However, is it realistic?

I once worked for a telecommunications company that tried a "boil the ocean" approach, where our first deliverable would be an organization-wide set of terms and definitions. After many years of working towards this goal and not producing any smaller yet still valuable deliverables, the entire effort was cancelled. The scope was too broad, and the business experts that were needed to validate terms and definitions for areas outside the immediate initiative were not readily available because there was no incentive from management for them to participate. In addition, time passes and the world changes, including changes to terms and meanings.

Limiting ourselves to an initiative reduces our scope and our time to complete, therefore increasing our chances for success. This smaller scope can in any case be a stepping stone to reaching an organization-wide Common Business Language. For example, Chips Inc. would like to centralize purchasing first and then payroll. Although we would prefer to set our scope wide and create a common set of terms and definitions across all of Chips Inc., or at least both purchasing and payroll, starting with purchasing would be a broad-enough scope to provide value. The term **Cookie** is within the scope of purchasing yet **Employee** would be out of scope until we focus on the payroll initiative.

The scope can be organization-wide or close to organization-wide if the initiative is very broad, such as introducing a vendor package to replace multiple legacy applications. Even with such a large project, however, there is a sequence to how processes get implemented, and it is to your advantage to scope the work in a similar sequence to demonstrate value each step of the way.

The drawback to choosing a smaller scope is that sometimes we have to go back later and revisit terms and definitions. We might agree on the definition of **Supplier** for the purchasing initiative, for example, but it is possible that payroll may view **Supplier** differently. Payroll might use the term **Vendor** and there might be subtle differences between **Supplier** and **Vendor**. This scenario will be resolved in one of these three ways:

1. Payroll will conform and use the purchasing perspective. The purchasing perspective on **Supplier** will become the Common Business Language term for referring to supplier and therefore payroll will use this same name and meaning.

2. Purchasing will need to change its perspective. Payroll might raise some really important points about a **Supplier** that will make us go back and update the meaning of a **Supplier** for everyone.

3. We will need to maintain a mapping. Both purchasing and payroll will maintain separate

perspectives and we will create a mapping so that they can speak with each other (Rosedata Stone).

Precise

Precision means "exactly or sharply defined or stated." As it relates to achieving a Common Business Language, precision is the naming, defining, and relating of a term so that it can be understood only one way and not more than one way.

Precision does not mean there is only one name and meaning for a term. For example, Bakery A can still call it a **Cookie**, Bakery B can call it a **Biscuit**, and Corporate can call it a **Cookie**. Corporate's definition of **Cookie** though, if it is the Common Business Language term, must be clear enough to only be read and understood one way.

Making terms precise is hard work. We need to transform the ambiguity in our verbal and sometimes written communication into a form where five people can read about the term and each get a single clear picture of the term, not five different interpretations. For example, a group of business users initially define **Product** as:

Something we produce intending to sell for profit.

Is this definition precise? If you and I read this definition, are we each clear on what *something* means? Is *something* tangible like a hammer or instead some type of service? If it is a hammer and we donate this hammer to a not-for-profit organization, is it still a hammer? After all, we didn't make a *profit* on it. The word *intending* may cover us, but still, shouldn't this word be explained in more detail? And who is *we*? Is it our entire organization or maybe just a subset? What does *profit* really mean anyway? Can two people read the word *profit* and see it very differently?

You see the problem. We need to think like a detective to find gaps and ambiguous statements in the text to make terms precise. After some debate, our **Product** definition is updated:

A product, also known as a finished product, is something that is in a state to be sold to a consumer. It has completed the manufacturing process, contains a wrapper, and is labeled for resale. A product is different than a raw material and a semi-finished good. A raw material such as sugar or milk, and a semi-finished good such as melted chocolate is never sold to a consumer. If in the future, sugar or milk is sold directly to consumers, than sugar and milk become products.

Examples:
Widgets Dark Chocolate 42 oz
Lemonizer 10 oz
Blueberry pickle juice 24 oz

Ask at least five people to see if they are all clear on this particular initiative's definition of a product. The best way to test precision is to try to break the definition. Think of lots of examples and see if everyone makes the same decision as to whether the examples are products or not.

Although our examples of precision have been focused on the meanings of terms, precision is equally important for the naming of terms.

I once worked with an insurance company whose employees were told to use **Product** instead of **Policy**. This was a bad idea because **Product** is so much broader and vaguer than **Policy**. A **Product** can be a **Policy** but can also be a YouTube video ad produced by this insurance company. Is this what the insurance company intended with introducing this name?

Precision is so important in how organizations work. For example, my wife works as a first responder in our town. Earlier this year, a 911 call reported that someone was having a heart attack at our park. Due to a lack of precision regarding where this person was located within the park—there were several park entrances—the ambulance team spent 30 minutes trying to find the person, and by the time the person was found it was too late.

William Mayo, CIO at the Broad Institute of MIT and Harvard said:

The ability to apply algorithms in real time at finely granulated levels to find previously hidden patterns and insights all depends on having an excellent understanding of the question you are asking and the nature of data.[5]

"Having an excellent understanding of the question you are asking" requires having a precise explanation of the terms in the question. If we do not all have the same understanding of **Product** for example, a simple question like, "How many products do we have?" is no longer so simple to answer.

In my consulting and training, I witness every organization I work with grappling with making terms precise.

In 1967, G.H. Mealy wrote a white paper where he made this statement:

> We do not, it seems, have a very clear and commonly agreed upon set of notions about data—either what they are, how they should be fed and cared for, or their relation to the design of programming languages and operating systems.[6]

---

[5] https://insights.techreview.com/excelling-in-the-new-data-economy/.

[6] G. H. Mealy, "Another Look at Data," AFIPS, pp. 525-534, 1967 Proceedings of the Fall Joint Computer Conference, 1967.

Although Mr. Mealy made this claim over 50 years ago, if we replace *programming languages and operating systems* with the word *databases* or *datastores*, we can make a similar claim today.

Aiming for precision can help us better understand our data and by extension our business terms.

A first step in solving a problem is to understand what caused it in the first place. In my data modeling classes, I use the *Precision Diamond*[7] to establish the one or more causes for a lack of precision for a particular initiative.

Diamond

There are four factors that lead to having multiple names and meanings for the same term. We will use **Customer** as an example in illustrating what I have created and called the *Precision Diamond*. According to the Experian Global Data Management Research Report, the strongest drivers for achieving a single view of Customer are to:[8]

---

http://tw.rpi.edu/media/2013/11/11/134fa/GHMealy-1967-FJCC-p525.pdf.

[7] *Data Modeling Master Class Training Manual*, 8th Edition, 2019, Technics Publications.

[8] *2019 Experian Global Data Management Research Report.* https://bit.ly/36JjJdL.

- Improve customer experience: 42%
- Improve operational efficiency: 38%
- Improve strategic decisions: 37%
- Increase customer retention: 36%
- Increase customer sales: 36%
- Reduce costs: 33%

If we can identify the factors that are driving each particular situation, we can address them and reach term precision. Let's discuss the four factors of context, time, motive, and state.

The Precision Diamond

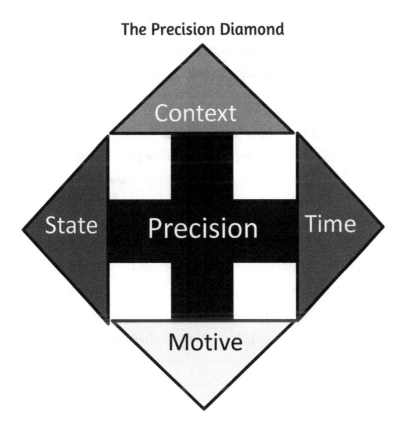

Context

Each of us approaches an initiative with a set of boundaries. I might look at the initiative limited by a marketing scope and you might look at the same initiative with a sales scope. Scope or context is the perspective with which each party views the term. **Customer** may be ambiguous because of context differences such as these:

- **Department versus organization**. The marketing department considers prospects to be customers but senior management does not.

- **Department versus department**. The marketing department considers prospects to be customers but the sales department considers only those who have placed orders to be customers.

- **Organization versus vendor package**. Senior management does not consider prospects to be customers, but the new CRM vendor package does.

A few years back I worked with a large federal agency. During the project, I uncovered an incredible amount of ambiguity in how terms were being named, used, and defined. For example, there were 26 different definitions for a **Facility**! Here are two real examples of these definitions, with department names changed to A and B:

Term	Department	Definition
commercial waste management facility	A	A treatment, storage, disposal, or transfer facility that accepts wastes from a variety of sources for profit. A commercial facility manages a broader spectrum of wastes than a private facility, which normally manages a limited volume or type of waste.
commercial waste management facility	B	A treatment, storage, disposal, or transfer facility which accepts waste from a variety of sources, as compared to a private facility which normally manages a limited waste stream generated by its own operations.

There is a department versus department context issue with these two definitions, especially when it comes to profit. Department A states that a commercial waste management facility accepts waste for profit but Department B does not consider profit in defining **Facility**.

We must resolve differences like this before we know what a **Facility** really is.

Time

And then there's change. Even after consensus has been reached on what things are to be represented in the information system, the impact of change must be considered. How much change can something undergo and still be the "same thing"?

...Suppose you and I start trading parts of our cars—tires, wheels, transmissions, suspensions, etc. At some point we will have exchanged cars, in the sense that the Department of Motor Vehicles must change their records as to who owns which car—but when? What is the "thing" which used to be my car, and when did you acquire it?[9]

This eloquent summary from *Data and Reality* emphasizes that terms can change over time. **Customer** may be ambiguous because of time:

- **Today versus the past**. For example, 15 years ago **Customer** might not have encompassed individuals and only included organizations, but today individuals are included.

- **Today versus the future**. For example, 15 years from now, **Customer** will include not just individuals and organizations, but also alien life forms—I know, too much *Star Trek*.

From the time of the Gutenberg Bible up to about 20 years ago, this definition for a book would have sufficed:

A book is factually defined as a written or printed work consisting of pages glued or sewn together along one

---

[9] *Data and Reality: A Timeless Perspective on Perceiving and Managing Information in Our Imprecise World*, 3rd ed., William Kent, Technics Publications, 2012.

side and bound in covers that communicates information.[10]

However, with eBooks and audio books this definition may no longer suffice.

Motive

Of the four factors that lead to having different names for the same term, motive can be the most difficult to uncover and the most difficult to resolve. There may be hidden reasons of prestige or income that lead people to name or define a term a certain way. Adding precision when motives are at stake can lead to someone losing something that they don't want to lose.

I worked with a large manufacturing company that had two different perspectives on a key sales figure. The accounting perspective wanted the number to be as small as possible to reduce taxes, and the sales team wanted the number to be as large as possible to maximize commissions. The money motive can be a difficult perspective to change.

State

People may view a term at a certain point in that term's lifecycle. **Customer** may be ambiguous because of state (also known as lifecycle). For example, a **Customer** starts

---

[10] https://bit.ly/2OdseqP.

off as a **Prospect**. This can lead to ambiguity as some may include **Prospect** in the meaning of a **Customer** whereas others do not.

To illustrate lifecycle issues, I did an assignment with a large university in California which could not come to agreement on what a **Student** is. I've since learned this is a common challenge with universities. This lack of precision in defining **Student** was due to state issues. The admissions department had a very different definition for **Student** than alumni affairs, for example. The admissions department included high school seniors in their definition. That is, those that have applied to the school. Whereas alumni affairs only considered those that had a degree from this university to be **Students**.

Minimal

We can maintain precision yet also only show what is meaningful to show. Precision does not require showing all of the details—instead only showing enough to enable understanding the terms just one way. We might know quite a bit of descriptive information about **Customer**, such as their name, birth date, and email address. This descriptive information, called properties or attributes, is too granular to capture in a BTM. Our focus needs to be on **Customer** and not **Customer First Name**, for example.

I worked with a team this past year at a large consumer product goods manufacturer. Our scope was finance. There were many financial measurements that were important, such as **Profit, Return on Total Assets,** and **Debt.** However, we needed to view finance at a much higher level because the higher level is where precision was needed. We tackled terms such as **Legal Entity** and **Business Unit,** as these needed to be named and defined consistently throughout the organization. After we have precision at this higher level, we were able move on to more details such as the finance measurements that might appear on a profit and loss statement.

Visuals

Remember the saying, "a picture is worth a thousand words?" It really is true. We need a diagram or figure that displays our terms. We might read an entire document but not reach that moment of clarity until we see a figure or picture summarizing everything. We humans are very visual animals, and we need to make sure we see things in picture form instead of text to make the most of communication. Words are processed 60,000 times slower than pictures.[11]

---

[11] https://mouthmedia.com/blog/the-power-of-visuals-over-words/.

Too often we see things in text. For example, my daughter was preparing for a test on aerobic respiration while I was drafting this chapter. Her notes were just text, her handwriting describing the phases of aerobic respiration including the inputs and outputs of each phase. It was so difficult to follow along with the text. I eventually Googled aerobic respiration and found this graphic:

Aerobic respiration

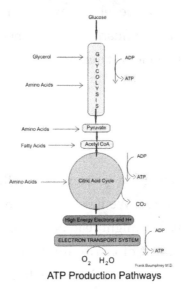

ATP Production Pathways

12

This made it much easier for her and me to understand the process of creating energy.

---

12 https://commons.wikimedia.org/wiki/File:Aerobic_pathways.png.

Takeaways

- Precision means there is only one interpretation for a term. This includes the term's name, definition, and or relationships to other terms. Most issues organizations face related to growth, credibility, and saving lives, stem from a lack of precision.

- The Precision Diamond reveals the four sources for imprecision: context, time, motive, and state.

- Minimal means showing only enough detail to enable understanding the terms just one way.

- Visuals means that we need a picture instead of lots of text. "A picture is worth a thousand words."

Chapter 3

Solution

After lunch later in the week, you return to Chips Inc.'s flagship bakery to treat yourself to another free chocolate chip cookie. You try to avoid getting distracted by the delicious smells of the pastries, and after finishing your cookie, you introduce yourself to the bakery staff and learn who is in charge of purchasing for this bakery.

It is a quiet day at the bakery, and she sits down with you for enough time for the following BTM to be completed along with definitions for each term.

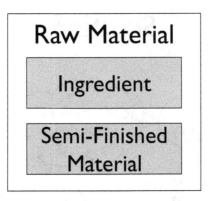

Term	Definition
Raw Material	A material used in creating bakery items that is either a semi-finished material or an ingredient. For example, to create a cake, the ingredients sugar and milk are needed, and the semi-finished materials of frosting and fondant are needed.
Ingredient	A material used in creating bakery items that, from the perspective of the bakery purchaser, cannot be broken down into smaller pieces. For example, to create a cake, the ingredients sugar and milk are needed.
Semi-finished Material	A material used in creating bakery items that, from the perspective of the bakery purchaser, contains multiple ingredients. For example, to create a cake, the semi-finished materials of frosting and fondant are needed. Frosting contains the ingredients of powdered sugar, cream, butter, and vanilla. Fondant contains the ingredients of sugar, water, and corn syrup.

This BTM is well-scoped, precise, minimal, and visual—recall the four needs discussed in the previous chapter. We did not choose to tackle all of the bakery terms; our scope included just these three. There is only one way to read this model—the names and definitions are unambiguous and therefore not up for interpretation, making the model precise. Only minimal information appears. We could have included properties such as **Raw Material Name** and **Raw Material Description**, but this additional information adds complexity without additional value. The diagram is also a powerful visual.

This chapter introduces the BTM as a precise, minimal, and visual tool scoped for a particular initiative. BTM components are explained as well, so you can read models like the one above. Experience the variations of relational and dimensional business terms models, and see how several data modeling tools display the BTM, including CaseTalk, ER/Studio, erwin DM, and Hackolade.

Models

While drafting this chapter, I needed to travel to Manhattan for a meeting. I exited the subway in Times Square at rush hour. It was dark and there were people and cars everywhere. I wasn't sure which way to walk—which way do street numbers go down or avenue numbers go up? Sensory overload!

I opened Google Maps on my phone and typed in the destination address. The map stripped away all of the complexities around me such as crowds, cars, and buildings, and just displayed a simple picture that helped me navigate.

The map is a powerful model.

A model is a language of symbols and text which simplifies a subset of the real world by only including representations of what we need to understand. Much is filtered out on a model, creating a 'fake,' but extremely useful, reflection of reality.

We need to 'speak' a language before we can discuss content. That is, once we know how to read the symbols on a model (syntax), we can discuss what the symbols represent (semantics). Once we understand the syntax, we can discuss the semantics.

We make use of models on a regular basis.

For example, a map helps a visitor navigate a city. Once we know what the symbols mean on a map, such as lines representing streets and blue representing water, we can read the map and use it as a valuable navigation tool for understanding a geographical landscape.

Map of a geographic landscape

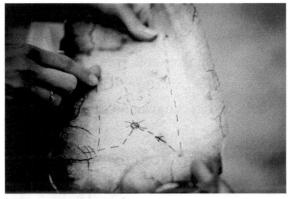

An organization chart helps an employee understand reporting relationships. The org chart contains representations too, such as boxes representing people and lines representing reporting relationships. Once we know what the boxes and lines mean on an organization chart, we can understand management reporting relationships and the organizational landscape.

Map of organizational landscape

A blueprint helps an architect communicate building plans. The blueprint, too, contains only representations, such as rectangles for rooms and lines for pipes. Once we know what the rectangles and lines mean on a blueprint, we know what the structure will look like and can understand the architectural landscape.

Map of architectural landscape

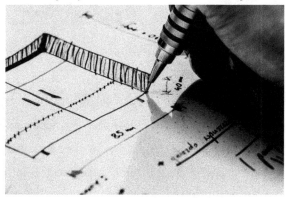

The business terms model helps business and IT professionals understand terms along with their definitions and connections. The BTM, too, contains only representations, such as rectangles for terms and lines for connections. Once we know what the rectangles and lines mean on a BTM, we can debate and eventually agree on the terms along with their meanings and connections, and therefore understand the informational landscape.

Map of informational landscape

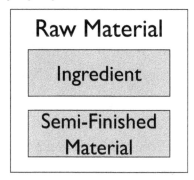

BTMs

Refining our focus from models in general to the BTM:

> *A BTM is a language of symbols and text which simplifies an informational landscape by providing a precise, minimal, and visual tool scoped for a particular initiative and tailored for a particular audience.*

This definition includes the needs of being well-scoped, precise, minimal, and visual. Knowing the type of visual that will have the greatest effectiveness requires knowing the audience for the model.

The audience includes the people who will validate and use the model. Validate means telling us whether the model is correct or needs adjustments. Use means reading and benefiting from the model. The scope encompasses an initiative, such as an application development project or a business intelligence program.

Knowing the audience and scope helps us decide which terms to model, what the terms mean, how the terms relate to each other, and what type of visual would have the greatest benefit. Additionally, knowing the scope ensures we don't "boil the ocean" and model every possible term, but instead only focus on those that will add value to our current initiative.

A BTM often fits nicely on a single piece of paper—and I don't mean plotter-size paper! Limiting a BTM to one page is important because it encourages us to select only key terms. We can fit 20 terms on one page but not 500 terms.

Being well-scoped, precise, minimal, and visual, the BTM provides a Common Business Language. We can capture and communicate complex and encompassing business processes and requirements, enabling people with different backgrounds and roles to initially discuss and debate terms, and to eventually communicate effectively using these terms.

Components

The three components of a BTM are terms, relationships, and definitions.

Terms

A term is a noun which represent a collection of business data and is considered both basic and critical to your audience for a particular initiative. Basic means this term is mentioned frequently in conversations in discussing the initiative. Critical means the initiative would be very different or non-existent without this term.

The majority of terms are easy to identify and include nouns that are common across industries, such as **Customer**, **Employee**, and **Product**. Terms can have different names and meanings within departments, organizations, or industries based on audience and initiative (scope). An airline may call a **Customer** a *Passenger*, a hospital may call a **Customer** a *Patient*, an insurance company may call a **Customer** a *Policyholder*, yet they are all recipients of goods or services.

Each term fits into one of six categories: who, what, when, where, why, or how. That is, each term is either a who, what, when, where, why, or how. The table on the next page contains a definition of each of these categories along with examples.

Terms are shown as rectangles in a BTM, such as these two for our bakery example:

Cookie		Ingredient

Category	Definition	Examples
Who	Person or organization of interest to the initiative.	Employee, Patient, Player, Suspect, Customer, Vendor, Student, Passenger, Competitor, Author
What	Product or service of interest to the initiative. What the organization makes or provides that keeps it in business.	Product, Service, Raw Material, Finished Good, Course, Song, Photograph, Tax Preparation, Policy, Cookie
When	Calendar or time interval of interest to the initiative.	Schedule, Semester, Fiscal Period, Duration
Where	Location of interest to the initiative. Location can refer to actual places as well as electronic places.	Employee Home Address, Distribution Point, Customer Website
Why	Event or transaction of interest to the initiative.	Order, Return, Complaint, Withdrawal, Payment, Trade, Claim
How	Documentation of the event of interest to the initiative. Records events such as a Purchase Order (a "How") recording an Order event (a "Why"). A document provides evidence that an event took place.	Invoice, Contract, Agreement, Purchase Order, Speeding Ticket, Packing Slip, Trade Confirmation

Term instances are the occurrences, examples, or values of a particular term. The term **Cookie** may have multiple instances such as chocolate chip, peanut butter, and sugar cookies. The term **Ingredient** may have multiple instances such as sugar, flour, and peanuts.

Relationships

A relationship represents a business connection between two terms, and is shown on the BTM as a line connecting these two terms. For example, here is a relationship between **Cookie** and **Ingredient**:

The word Contain is called a *label*. A label adds meaning to the relationship. Instead of just saying that a **Cookie** must relate to an **Ingredient**, we can say that a **Cookie** must contain **Ingredients**. "Contain" is more meaningful than "relate."

A relationship can either represent a business rule or a navigation path, depending on the purpose of the model.

If the goal of the initiative is to capture how a business process works, in anticipation of introducing, replacing, integrating, or customizing an operational application, then the rules governing the terms are very important to understand and capture. For example, the relationship between **Cookie** and **Ingredient** captures the business rule that a **Cookie** must contain **Ingredients**. The type of BTM that captures rules is called *relational*.

If the goal of the initiative is to capture how well a business process is performing in anticipation of introducing, replacing, integrating, or customizing an analytical application, then the quantitative questions that need to be answered as part of the analytics initiative are very important to identify and capture. For example, if we would like to know how well the purchasing process is doing, we might identify these quantitative questions as important to answer:

1. How much in ingredients did we purchase this quarter across all of our bakeries?
2. How much in ingredients did Bakery A spend last quarter?
3. How much did we spend for all ingredients for all bakeries during March 2020?

The type of BTM that captures navigation paths to answer quantitative questions such as these is called *dimensional*. Here is an example of a dimensional BTM that can answer these three questions on purchasing performance:

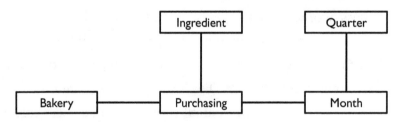

This dimensional BTM allows us to view purchasing at different levels of granularity, such as for a particular **Bakery, Ingredient,** and **Month**. We can also view purchasing for a particular **Bakery, Ingredient,** and **Quarter** by navigating from **Month** up to **Quarter**.

A dimensional BTM does not contain relationship labels like the relational. Each relationship line on a dimensional exists purely to help with navigation and not capture a business rule, which is where labels would be used.

To summarize, when there is a need to understand how processes work, we care about the rules and will therefore build a relational BTM. When there is a need to understand how processes are performing, we care about the quantitative questions and will therefore build a dimensional BTM.

We will explore relational and dimensional BTMs in greater detail later in this chapter and also through the remainder of the book. Let's now return to relationships.

So far we know that a relationship represents a business connection between two terms. It would be nice to know more about the relationship such as whether a **Cookie** may contain many **Ingredients**, or whether an **Ingredient** may be used in baking many **Cookies**. This is where cardinality comes in.

Cardinality

Cardinality are additional symbols on the relationship line which communicate how many instances from one term participate in the relationship with instances of the other term. For example, on the relationship between **Cookie** and **Ingredient**, cardinality can show how many **Cookies** contain a particular **Ingredient**, and how many **Ingredients** are used to bake a particular **Cookie**.

There are several modeling notations, and each notation has its own set of symbols. Throughout this book, we use a notation called *Information Engineering*. The IE notation has been a very popular notation since the early 1980s. If you are using a notation other than IE within your organization, you will need to translate the symbols into the corresponding symbols in your modeling notation. We will see examples of other notations shortly.

For cardinality, we can choose any combination of zero, one, or many. *Many* (some people use "more") means any number greater than one. Specifying one or many allows us to capture *how many* of a particular term instance participates in a given relationship. Specifying zero or one allows us to capture whether a term instance is or is not required in a relationship.

Recall this relationship between **Cookie** and **Ingredient**:

Let's now add cardinality.

We need to ask what I call *Participation* questions to learn more. Participation questions tell us whether the relationship is 'one' or 'many'. So for example:

- Can a **Cookie** contain more than one **Ingredient**?
- Can an **Ingredient** be used in baking more than one **Cookie**?

A simple spreadsheet can keep track of these questions and their answers:

Question	Yes	No
Can a Cookie contain more than one Ingredient?		
Can an Ingredient be used in baking more than one Cookie?		

We ask the bakery purchaser and receive these answers:

Question	Yes	No
Can a Cookie contain more than one Ingredient?	✓	
Can an Ingredient be used in baking more than one Cookie?	✓	

We learn that a **Cookie** can contain more than one **Ingredient** such as sugar and flour. We also learn that an **Ingredient** such as sugar can be used in baking multiple cookies, such as in baking chocolate chip cookies and peanut butter cookies. So a **Cookie** can contain many **Ingredients** and an **Ingredient** can be used in baking many **Cookies**. 'Many' on a data model in the IE notation is a symbol which looks like a crow's foot (and is called a *crow's foot* by data folks):

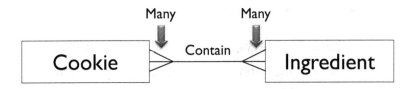

Now we know more about the relationship:

- Each **Cookie** contains many **Ingredients**.
- Each **Ingredient** is used in baking many **Cookies**.

I also always use the word 'each' in reading a relationship, and start with the term that makes the most sense to the reader, usually the one that has the clearest relationship label. Bakers may think a **Cookie** would be a better starting point than an **Ingredient**, for example, in reading the relationship. Be flexible, and start with the side that makes the most sense.

This relationship is not yet precise, though. In addition to asking these two Participation questions, we also need to ask what I call the *Existence* questions. Existence tells us for each relationship whether one term can exist without the other term. For example:

- Can a **Cookie** exist without **Ingredients?**
- Can an **Ingredient** exist without **Cookies?**

We ask the bakery experts and receive these answers:

Question	Yes	No
Can a Cookie exist without Ingredients?		✓
Can an Ingredient exist without Cookies?	✓	

So we learn that a **Cookie** cannot exist without **Ingredients**. This means for example, that a chocolate chip cookie must have at least one **Ingredient**. In addition, we learn that you can have **Ingredients** that are not used in baking **Cookies**. Maybe frosting for example, is an ingredient the bakery uses on **Cakes** but not **Cookies**.

Here is what the answers to these two questions would look like on the model:

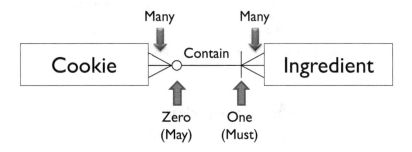

After adding existence, we have a precise relationship:

- Each **Cookie** must contain many **Ingredients**.
- Each **Ingredient** may be used in baking many **Cookies**.

I also call the Existence questions the May/Must questions. The Existence questions tell us when reading the relationship, whether we say "may" or "must." A zero means "may", indicating optionality—the entity can exist without the other entity. **Ingredients** *may* be used in baking **Cookies**, for example. A one means "must", indicating required—the entity cannot exist without the other entity. **Cookie** *must* contain **Ingredients**, for example.

So to summarize, the Participation questions reveal whether each entity has a one or many relationship to the other entity. The Existence questions reveal whether each entity has an optional ("may") or mandatory ("must") relationship to the other entity.

If participation and existence are not yet clear, don't worry. We will practice through many more examples. In addition, the more BTMs you create, the easier it will become to think of participation and existence for each relationship.

Use instances to make things clear in the beginning, and eventually to help when you explain your BTMs to colleagues. On this model for example:

We can use this sample dataset:

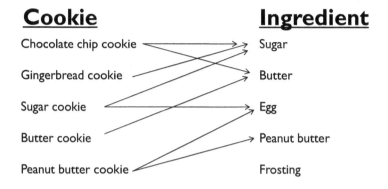

Cookie   Ingredient

Although I like to eat cookies, I am a not good baker—though I can make a mean peanut butter and jelly sandwich. I don't have the correct ingredients above, but it is an illustration of cardinality in our model. Our model shows that a **Cookie** must contain one or many **Ingredients** and you can see that all of the **Cookies** above contain at least one **Ingredient**. In addition, we know from our model that each **Ingredient** may be used in baking many **Cookies**. And you can see that here too. All of the **Ingredients** are used in baking at least one **Cookie** except for frosting.

Answering all four questions leads to a precise relationship. Precise means we all read the model the same exact way. For example, here are just a few of the questions we can answer with our precise model:

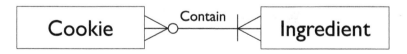

- Can a cookie contain multiple ingredients? *Yes, a cookie can contain sugar, flour, etc.*

- Can an ingredient belong to more than one cookie? *Yes, an ingredient can be used in baking many cookies such as peanut butter cookies and chocolate chip cookies.*

- Can a chocolate chip cookie exist without any ingredients? *No, you must have at least one ingredient in a chocolate chip cookie.*

- Can an ingredient exist without a cookie? *Yes, some ingredients are only for cakes such as frosting.*

Let's look at two more terms, **Supplier** and **Ingredient**:

Supplier		Ingredient

We learn that there is a business connection between these two terms. A **Supplier** may provide **Ingredients**:

Supplier	Provide	Ingredient

We then ask our Participation questions:

Question	Yes	No
Can a Supplier provide more than one Ingredient?	✓	
Can an Ingredient be provided by more than one Supplier?		✓

Our model now looks like this:

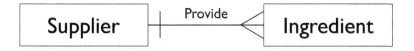

Next we ask our Existence questions:

Question	Yes	No
Can a Supplier exist without Ingredients?	✓	
Can an Ingredient exist without Suppliers?		✓

Our model now gets updated to this:

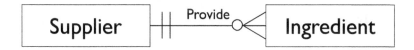

And we would read this model like this:

- Each **Supplier** may provide many **Ingredients**.
- Each **Ingredient** must be provided by one **Supplier**.

This relationship tells us that some **Suppliers** may not provide any **Ingredients**. How can this be? Maybe we have **Suppliers** that we are evaluating and we call them *suppliers* but they have not yet supplied us with **Ingredients**.

Always jot down some instances on a white board or flipchart if you think your audience is having trouble understanding cardinality:

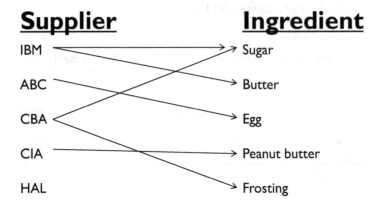

Each **Supplier** may provide many **Ingredients**, and we can see this with IBM providing two **Ingredients**, ABC with just one **Ingredient**, CBA with two **Ingredients**, CIA with one **Ingredient**, and HAL with no **Ingredients**. Each **Ingredient** must be provided by one **Supplier**, and we see this here as well.

Wait a minute! Sugar is provided by both IBM and CBA. Our model says this cannot happen. Either our dataset is incorrect or the model needs to be updated.

We can use our BTM to determine whether an **Ingredient** can be provided by more than one **Supplier**. BTMs speak in facts and exactness. Let's get right to the point and debate. Lawyers and police officers often speak and write with precision that would make them great modelers (politicians, on the other hand …).

So let's assume the previous dataset was wrong and IBM is the only supplier of sugar:

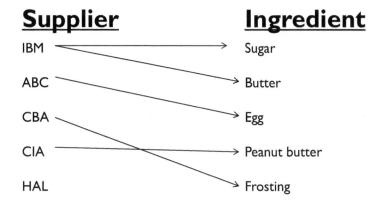

The relationship between **Cookie** and **Ingredient** is an example of a many-to-many relationship, as a **Cookie** must contain many **Ingredients**, and an **Ingredient** may be used in baking many **Cookies**.

The relationship between **Supplier** and **Ingredient** is a one-to-many relationship as a **Supplier** may provide many **Ingredients**, and an **Ingredient** must be provided by one **Supplier**.

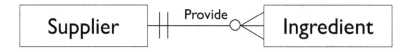

Be very clear on labels. Labels are the verbs that connect our terms (nouns), and to read any complete sentence we need both nouns and verbs. Sometimes a different label can impact the answers to the Participation and Existence questions. For example, if the relationship between **Supplier** and **Ingredient** is Deliver instead of Provide, the answers to the four questions may be very different.

Make sure the labels on the relationship lines are as descriptive as possible. Here are some examples of good labels:

- Contain
- Provide
- Own
- Initiate
- Categorize

Avoid the following words as labels, as they provide no additional information to the reader. You can use these words in combination with other words to make a meaningful label; just avoid using these words by themselves:

- Have
- Associate
- Participate
- Relate
- Are

For example, replace the relationship sentence:

"Each **Suppler** may *be associated with* many **Ingredients**."

With:

"Each **Suppler** may *provide* many **Ingredients**."

Subtyping

A very powerful communication symbol for the BTM is the subtyping relationship. The subtyping relationship is used to group common terms together. For example, the **Student** and **Teacher** terms might be grouped using subtyping under the more generic **Person** term. In this example, **Person** would be called the grouping term or supertype and **Student** and **Teacher** would be the terms that are grouped together, also known as the subtypes:

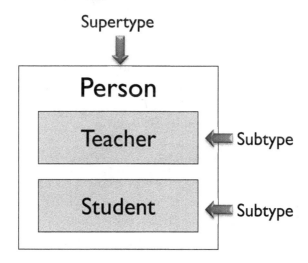

We would read this model as:

- Each **Person** may be either a **Teacher** or a **Student**.
- **Teacher** is a **Person**.
- **Student** is a **Person**.

The subtyping relationship means that all of the relationships connected to the supertype from other terms are inherited to each subtype. Therefore, the relationships to **Person** also belong to **Teacher** and **Student**. So for example, on this BTM, the relationship to **Car** also belongs to **Teacher** and **Student**:

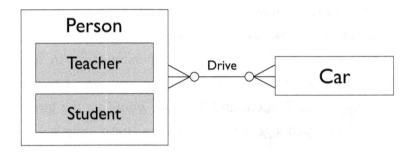

So the relationship:

- Each **Person** may drive many **Cars**.
- Each **Car** may be driven by many **People**.

Also applies to **Teacher** and **Student**:

- Each **Teacher** may drive many **Cars**.
- Each **Car** may be driven by many **Teachers**.

- Each **Student** may drive many **Cars**.
- Each **Car** may be driven by many **Students**.

Not only does subtyping reduce redundancy on a data model, but it makes it easier to communicate similarities across what otherwise would appear to be distinct and separate terms.

Subtyping just groups common terms together but does not imply they are related. For example, **Teacher** and **Student** in the model above do not have a relationship. We would need to create a relationship between **Teacher** and **Student** if there is a connection between them, such as:

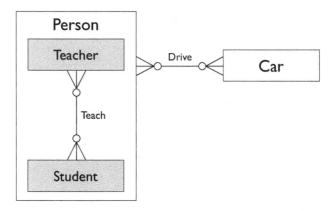

- Each **Teacher** may teach many **Students**.
- Each **Student** may be taught by many **Teachers**.

Mapping

The mapping relationship captures different perspectives of the same thing. Recall the visual appearing on the next page of the multiple ways of referring to a **Cookie**. Each arrow in this visual is a mapping relationship. We are capturing the relationship between a store's perspective and our Common Business Language.

A mapping is limited to a single term such as **Cookie**, and just like the Rosetta Stone, helps you speak multiple languages. Even if the individual stores never switch to the common term, we can still speak with them clearly using their terms.

Five Mapping Relationships

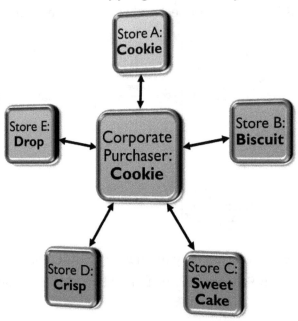

There is no standard way of representing these mappings—use the type of visual you know your audience would best understand.

Definitions

Although definitions are not shown on the visual, they are necessary for BTM precision. In addition, as you work with teams to refine the meanings of terms, you will often change, remove, and add terms and relationships.

We need to be aware of three characteristics that lead to a high-quality definition: clarity, completeness, and correctness. Clarity means that a reader can understand the meaning of a term by reading the definition only once. A clear definition does not require the reader to decipher how each sentence should be interpreted. Completeness means all of the necessary parts of the definition are present, such as examples and exceptions. Correctness means that an expert in the field would agree that the definition is accurate.

Definition Bingo

There is a game I sometimes play at my client sites called *Definition Bingo*. I use this game to determine both the perceived and actual quality of term definitions within the scope of the initiative.

Sample Definition Bingo card

B	I	N	G	O
Customer	Product	Account	Prospect	Calendar
Visit	Contract	Department	Credit	Citizen
Site	Order	★	Resource	Service
Employee	Agency	Consumer	Vehicle	Case
Organization	Facility	Expense	Project	Event

Just like the game of Bingo, there are cards and no two cards are identical. But in each cell there is a business term instead of having a number. If someone can prove that the organization has one clear definition for that term within the defined scope of the initiative, they can check off that cell. If they can complete a vertical, horizontal, or diagonal line, they yell "Bingo!" and win the game. Spoiler alert—I've never seen anyone win.

As mentioned, I worked for a government agency that managed facilities, and they had 26 different definitions for a **Facility**! I worked for a high-end automotive company that had over 20 different definitions for a **Vehicle**. Imagine a car company that has been around for over 100 years and they still do not collectively know what a **Vehicle** is!

Next time you stay at a hotel, ask the people at the front desk how they define **Visit**. Hotel business experts often cannot agree on what a **Visit** is. If someone stays during the week and pays with their corporate credit card and then stays for the weekend using their own personal credit card, is this one visit or two? If someone switches a room because of noise, is this one visit or two? If one person books three rooms is this one visit or three? Hospitals too, have difficulty defining a **Visit**. Someone gets admitted to the emergency room and then needs to go to three other medical departments—is this one visit or four? Marketing companies struggle with **Visit** too. Someone visits a webpage and then goes elsewhere and returns later that same day—is this one visit or two?

I know a skilled analyst in Australia who once did a consulting assignment for an Australian airline. This airline had two definitions for **Service**. You might think "Only two, that's not bad." However, one definition was from the maintenance crew where service meant that the aircraft is undergoing maintenance and something is being fixed. The other definition was from the flight crew where service meant that the plane is flying and transporting passengers. Imagine accidently swapping these two definitions for **Service**?

Here is a blank Definition Bingo card. Fill it in with terms you think your organization would have difficulty defining for your current initiative.

Definition Bingo card template

B	I N G	O
	★	

I bet this was an easy exercise to complete. That is, the terms that are the most ambiguous are also often the most important, and we think of these first.

Clear, complete, and correct

The following page contains an example of a good definition. What I like about this definition is that it is clear, complete, and correct.

Clear means you can read this definition just one time and know how **Customer** is defined for this initiative. For example, there are no obscure acronyms or strange unedited sentences. This definition, although containing many sentences, is simple to read and comprehend.

A Customer is a person or organization who obtains our product for resale. The Customer normally obtains the product through purchase. An example of a customer who does not purchase our product is the Salvation Army, which receives the product for free as a charity organization. A person or organization must have obtained at least one product from us to be considered a Customer. That is, Prospects are not Customers. Also, once a Customer, always a Customer so even Customers that have not obtained anything in 50 years are still considered Customers. The Customer is different than the Consumer, who obtains the product for consumption as opposed to resale.

Examples:
Walmart
Bob's Grocery Store
Military Base 1332

Complete means those vague terms are explained, such as the word "normally" in the second sentence. The third sentence provides the Salvation Army as an example of the exception described in the second sentence. Completeness in this definition includes how **Consumer** and **Prospect** are distinguished from **Customer**. Completeness also includes examples such as Walmart and Bob's Grocery Store. Showing examples is a fantastic way to explain terms.

Correctness means that someone with credibility on the business side has verified that the definition is accurate.

I am working with one organization now, where certain terms due to their importance and also potential for ambiguity have definitions almost two pages in length!

If the definitions behind the terms on a data model are nonexistent or poor, multiple interpretations of the term become a strong possibility and we lose precision. For example, let's say this structure appears on our BTM:

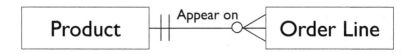

The relationship captures that:

- Each **Product** may appear on many **Order Lines**.
- Each **Order Line** must reference one **Product**.

You may look at this model and wonder "Does **Product** include **Research Items** not yet available for sale?" This is a valid question since the optionality symbol near **Order Line** tells us that certain **Products** have never been ordered. Maybe they have not been ordered because they are **Research Items** that are not yet available for sale.

Let's say you read the definition of **Product** hoping it will answer this question. If the definition for **Product** is missing or of poor quality and does not answer this question, you are left with making assumptions. I might have the same question as you and be forced to make an assumption as well. Now we are both making assumptions and if those assumptions are different from each other, we will read the same model different ways, which means that the data model is no longer a precise communication tool.

Variations

Recall that when there is a need to understand how processes work, we care about the rules and will therefore build a relational BTM. When there is a need to understand how processes are performing, we care about the quantitative questions and will therefore build a dimensional BTM.

Let's look at an example of each.

Relational

The model samples provided in the last section were relational. The relational BTM includes terms, their definitions, and the relationships that capture the business rules between these terms. Here is another example of a relational BTM:

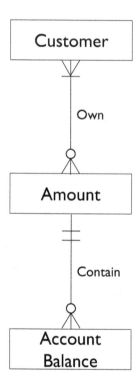

The relationships capture that:

- Each **Customer** may own many **Accounts**.
- Each **Account** must be owned by many **Customers**.

- Each **Account** may contain many **Account Balances**.
- Each **Account Balance** must belong to one **Account**.

We wrote the following definitions during one of our meetings with the project sponsor:

Customer	A customer is a person or organization who has opened one or more accounts with our bank. If members of a household each have their own account, each member of a household is considered a distinct customer. If someone has opened an account and then closed it, they are still considered a customer.
Account	An account is a contractual arrangement by which our bank holds funds on behalf of a customer.
Account Balance	An account balance is a financial record of how much money a customer has in a particular account with our bank at the end of a given time period such as someone's checking account balance at the end of a month.

Dimensional

To understand and document our analytical requirements, we can build a dimensional BTM such as the one on the next page. In this case, we'd like to know the performance of the fee generation process. For example, seeing the fees at a **Branch**, **Customer Category** (such as Individual or

Corporate), **Month,** and **Account Type** (such as Checking or Savings) level. This model also communicates the requirement to see fees not just at a **Month** level but also at a **Year** level, not just a **Branch** level, but also at a **Region** and **District** level.

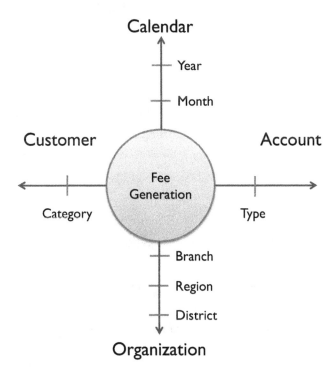

Term definitions:

Fee Generation	Fee generation is the business process where money is charged to customers for the privilege to conduct transactions against their account, or money charged based on time intervals such as monthly charges to keep a checking account open that has a low balance.

Branch	A branch is a physical location open for business. Customers visit branches to conduct transactions.
Region	A region is our bank's own definition of dividing a country into smaller pieces for branch assignment or reporting purposes.
District	A district is a grouping of regions used for organizational assignments or reporting purposes. Districts can and often do cross country boundaries, such as North America and Europe districts.
Customer Category	A customer category is a grouping of one or more customers for reporting or organizational purposes. Examples of customer categories are Individual, Corporate, and Joint.
Account Type	An account type is a grouping of one or more accounts for reporting or organizational purposes. Examples of account types are Checking, Savings, and Brokerage.
Year	A year is a period of time containing 365 days, consistent with the Gregorian calendar.
Month	A month is each of the twelve named periods into which a year is divided.

You might encounter terms such as **Year** and **Month** which are commonly understood terms and therefore minimal time can be invested in writing a definition. Make sure though that these are commonly understood terms, as sometimes even **Year** can have multiple meanings such as whether the reference is to a fiscal or standard calendar.

Fee Generation is an example of a meter. A meter represents a business process that is being measured. The meter is so important to the dimensional model that the name of the meter is often the name of the application: the **Sales** meter, the Sales Analytics Application.

District, Region, and **Branch** represent the levels of detail we can navigate within the **Organization** dimension. A *dimension* is a subject whose purpose is to add meaning to the measures. **Year** and **Month** represent the levels of detail we can navigate within the **Calendar** dimension. So this model contains four dimensions: **Organization, Calendar, Customer,** and **Account.**

Tools

Although a BTM displayed using PowerPoint or a similar drawing tool can be very effective, there are three advantages of using a professional data modeling tool for creating and sharing BTMs:

1. **Support.** Data modeling tool vendors often offer dedicated support desks. In addition, should there be an existing competency with a specific data modeling tool within your organization—for example, if your data management team is already using CaseTalk, ER/Studio, erwin DM, or Hackolade—you can then ask your colleagues for

help when you have questions on the tool. If your organization does not have a competency with any of these tools, your pioneering experience in using one or more of these tools can be very beneficial when it comes time to eventually evaluate and obtain multiple licenses for the data management team.

2. **Influence**. Professional data modeling tools offer lots of functionality to validate data models and integrate with other tools, such as process, glossary, catalog, and development tools, to increase the impact of your BTM throughout the organization.

3. **Design**. Once you build the BTM in this tool, information technology professionals, such as data architects and data modelers, can use your BTM file as the starting point for more detailed data modeling work within this tool, such as for creating logical and physical data models. This is because data modeling tools offer the functionality to go from BTM to detailed data models to eventually a database structure.

The model on the next page shows the two relationships we created earlier in this chapter—between **Cookie** and **Ingredient** and between **Supplier** and **Ingredient**—on one model.

Let's get a taste of how several powerful data modeling tools can represent this model. Tools are described in alphabetical order.

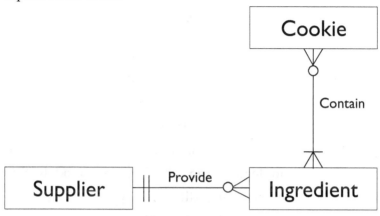

CaseTalk

We covered earlier in this chapter that multiple data modeling notations exist and that we are using Information Engineering in this book. A number of data modeling notations, including Fully Communication Oriented Information Modeling, FCO-IM, are grouped under the category of fact-based modeling. A fact is a business assertion, such as, "The chocolate chip cookie contains butter." Fact-based modeling is about identifying business assertions, called *facts*, and then grouping them into terms, called *fact types*, such as, "The chocolate chip cookie contains butter," leading to **Cookie** and **Ingredient** terms with a connecting relationship.

What I like about FCO-IM is that most initiative requirements fit nicely into a business assertion pattern. The purchaser at Bakery A for example, would probably use the word butter more often than the term **Ingredient**.

CaseTalk is the most popular tool that supports FCO-IM. Most data modeling tools were initially built with a particular type of database in mind, such as relational databases. However, FCO-IM is completely database-independent. Once the BTM is complete in CaseTalk, it can be expanded to logical and physical data models that eventually can generate different types of database structures such as spreadsheet, relational, XML, and JSON. So for our **Cookie, Ingredient**, and **Supplier** example, we would first need to identify the business assertions:

```
 1 ⊟ [EXPFILE]
 2   ; The cookie expressions are based upon the examples provided by Steve Hoberman.
 3   ; They are modeled using Fact Oriented Modeling in CaseTalk by Marco Wobben.
 4
 5 ⊟ [Ingredient]
 6   "Ingredient frosting exists."
 7
 8 ⊟ [Supplier]
 9   "Supplier HAL exists."
10
11 ⊟ [Ingredient Supplier]
12   "IBM supplies butter."
13   "IBM supplies sugar."
14   "ABC supplies egg."
15   "CBA supplies sugar."
16   "CBA supplies frosting."
17   "CIA supplies peanut butter."
18
19 ⊟ [Cookie Ingredient]
20   "The chocolate chip cookie contains butter."
21   "The chocolate chip cookie contains sugar."
22   "The peanut butter cookie contains sugar."
23   "The peanut butter cookie contains peanut butter."
24   "The sugar cookie contains peanut sugar."
25   "The sugar cookie contains egg."
26   "The butter cookie contains butter."
27   "The ginger bread cookie contains sugar."
28   "The ginger bread cookie contains egg."
29
30   |
```

Next we start grouping these assertions into terms and relationships:

"<Supplier> supplies <Ingredient>"

'<Supplier Name>'   '<Ingredient Name>'

CBA   sugar

Which then forms our BTM:

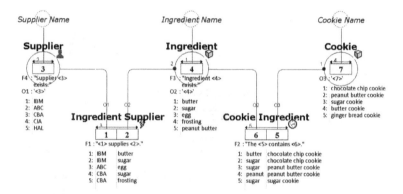

CaseTalk offers a lot of functionality that is beyond this overview, so visit https://www.casetalk.com/ to learn more and download a free trial.

ER/Studio

IDERA offers many data-related solutions including their ER/Studio Enterprise Team Edition, which is a powerful business-driven data architecture solution that combines multi-platform data modeling, design, and reporting with cross-organizational team collaboration. Enterprise Team Edition includes a number of tools including:

- **Data Architect**. This data modeling tool supports numerous notations. I use Data Architect for many projects including for the data modeling course I currently teach at Columbia University in their Applied Analytics program.

- **Business Architect**. This process modeling tool enables architects to create business process models. A shared repository between Data Architect and Business Architect means users can integrate between a BTM and a conceptual data flow diagram, for example.

- **Team Server**. This glossary and metadata tool provides a web user interface that allows both business and data stakeholders to collaborate on improving data modeling and metadata deliverables.

Data Architect is very intuitive to learn, and is similar in look and feel to products like Microsoft Word and navigation like Microsoft Explorer. It also contains a set of macros and powerful macro language to extend the functionality of the tool.

Here is our model in Data Architect:

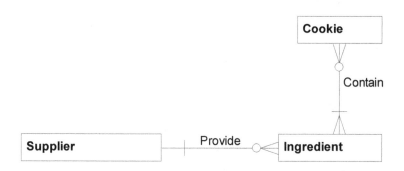

When there is just a single one symbol on the relationship line, it means a one for Participation and a must for Existence. An **Ingredient** must be provided by one **Supplier**.

To learn more and download a free trial, visit https://www.idera.com/.

erwin DM

erwin Data Modeler is a very powerful data modeling tool that supports numerous notations. I have used erwin since 1992 to build business term, logical, and physical data models, as well as in generating the underlying relational database structure from the physical data model.

The company, erwin, has several other tools that integrate with erwin DM and each other:

- **erwin DC**. erwin Data Catalog automates enterprise metadata management, data mapping, reference data management, data quality, code generation, data lineage, and impact analysis.

- **erwin DL**. erwin Data Literacy combines a glossary and user portal for viewing relevant data by user role.

- **erwin Evolve**. erwin Evolve is a full-featured, configurable set of enterprise architecture and business process modeling and analysis tools.

erwin DM is very easy to learn and use, and there are different versions available depending on how much modeling functionality is needed. The Standard and Workgroup Editions offer lots of functionality including collaboration tools and Complete Compare, which compares two structures for differences such as two BTMs or a physical model with a database design. The Workgroup Edition adds concurrent modeling, change management including versioning and conflict resolution, and granular model access control to assist in scaling your modeling practice across the enterprise. The Navigator Edition offers read-only access to the models.

Here is our model in erwin DM:

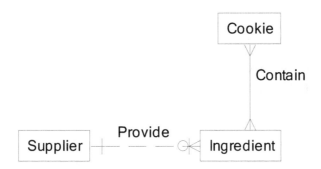

To learn more and download a free trial, visit https://www.erwin.com/.

Hackolade

More and more organizations are building software solutions that store data in NoSQL. NoSQL means that the database structure is not a relational database. For example, MongoDB, a NoSQL document database, stores data in JSON and not in the relational database structures of tables and columns.

Hackolade provides teams using NoSQL with a powerful visualization and database generation tool.

Hackolade is a data modeling tool built to handle complex types of data structures such as JSON. As a result, Hackolade is a very useful data modeling tool for NoSQL databases such as MongoDB, Neo4j, Cassandra, Couchbase, Cosmos DB, DynamoDB, Elasticsearch, HBase, Hive, Google BigQuery, Firebase/Firestore, MarkLogic,

Amazon Neptune, TinkerPop, ArangoDB, AWS Glue Data Catalog, Snowflake, as well as JSON stored in blobs of relational databases. In addition to modeling for databases, Hackolade can be used to model for communication protocols, such as for REST Application Programming Interfaces, plus Avro for Kafka and also the Parquet storage format.

Its visual component however, can also be used to create BTMs. For example, here are two versions of our BTM in Hackolade:

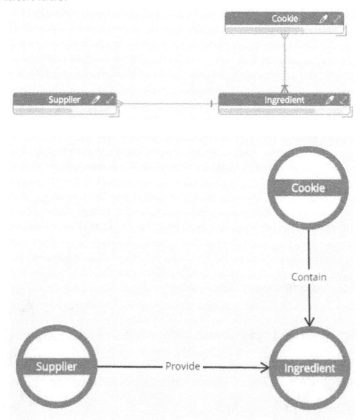

The first one provides a document perspective that eventually might lead to a NoSQL database which stores data in JSON, and the second one a graph perspective which eventually might lead to a NoSQL database which stores data in a property graph. Hackolade can generate both document and graph databases, and by just showing the document name or graph node name instead of all of the properties, we can create a BTM.

Which one of these two visuals should we use? We will cover in the next chapter how to choose a particular visual for a particular audience.

To learn more and download a free trial, visit https://www.hackolade.com/.

Takeaways

- A BTM is a language of symbols and text which simplifies an informational landscape by providing a precise, minimal, and visual tool scoped for a particular initiative and tailored for a particular audience.

- Once we know how to read the symbols on a model (syntax), we can discuss what the symbols represent (semantics).

- When there is a need to understand how processes work, we care about the rules and will therefore build a relational BTM. When there is a need to understand how processes are performing, we care about the quantitative questions and will therefore build a dimensional BTM.

- Play Definition Bingo to gauge the quality of the definitions for your initiative, and make sure all definitions are clear, complete, and correct.

- Use a mapping visual to translate a common term between multiple languages. Be flexible on the format you choose; think of your audience.

- Using a professional data modeling tool to create your BTM, such as CaseTalk, ER/Studio, erwin DM, or Hackolade, ensures sufficient tool support, increases BTM impact due to data modeling tool integration with other tools, and allows data professionals to use your BTM file as the starting point for more detailed data modeling work.

CHAPTER 4

Construction

"You put too much flour in that cake!"

This chapter covers the five steps for building a BTM for both operational (relational) and analytics (dimensional) initiatives.

Steps to create a BTM

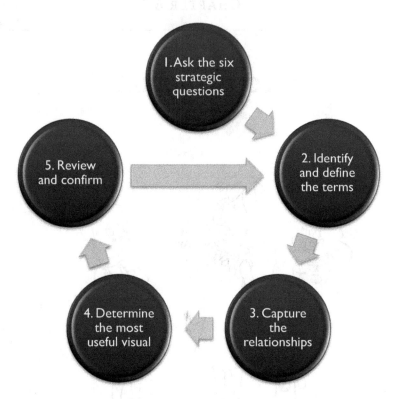

Before you begin any project, there are six strategic questions that must be asked (Step 1). These questions are a prerequisite to the success of any initiative because they ensure we choose the right terms for our BTM. Next, identify all terms within the scope of the initiative (Step 2). Make sure each term is clearly and completely defined. Then determine how these terms are related to each other (Step 3). Often, you will need to go back to Step 2 at this point, because in capturing relationships you may come up with new terms. Next, determine the most beneficial visual for your audience (Step 4). Consider the visual that would resonate best with those that will need to review and use your BTM. As a final step, seek approval of your BTM (Step 5). Often at this point there are additional changes to the model, and we cycle through these steps until the model is accepted.

Relational

Let's build a relational BTM following these five steps.

Step 1: Ask the six strategic questions

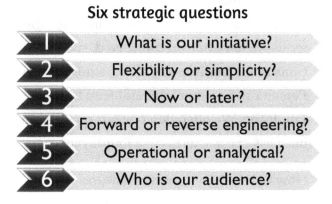

Six strategic questions

1. What is our initiative?
2. Flexibility or simplicity?
3. Now or later?
4. Forward or reverse engineering?
5. Operational or analytical?
6. Who is our audience?

There are six questions that need to be asked:

1. **What is our initiative?** This question ensures we know enough about the initiative to determine the

scope. Knowing the scope allows us to decide which terms should appear on the initiative's BTM. Eric Evans, in his book *Domain-Driven Design*, introduces the concept of "Bounded Context," which is all about understanding and defining your scope. If our scope is limited to purchasing, for example, **Raw Material** and **Supplier** would be within scope and **Sales** and **Promotion** most likely out of scope.

2. **Flexibility or simplicity?** This question ensures we introduce generic terms only if there is a need for flexibility. Generic terms allow us to accommodate new types of terms that we do not know about today and also allows us to better group similar terms together. For example, **Person** is flexible and **Employee** is simple. **Person** can include other terms we have not yet considered, such as **Consumer**, **Auditor**, and **Competitor**. However, **Person** can be a more difficult term to relate to than **Employee**. We often describe our processes using business-specific terms like **Employee**.

3. **Now or later?** This question ensures we have chosen the correct time perspective for our BTM. BTMs capture a Common Business Language at a point in time. If we are intent on capturing how business processes work or are analyzed today, then we need to make sure terms along with their

definitions and relationships reflect a current perspective (now). If we are intent on capturing how business processes work or are analyzed at some point in the future, such as one year or three years into the future, then we need to make sure terms along with their definitions and relationships reflect a future perspective (later).

4. **Forward or reverse engineering?** This question ensures we are selecting the most appropriate "language" for the BTM. If the initiative is being driven by business requirements, then it is a forward engineering effort and we choose a business language. It does not matter whether the organization is using SAP or Siebel, the BTM will contain business terms. If the initiative is being driven by an application, then it is a reverse engineering effort and we choose an application language. If the application uses the term **Object** for the term **Product**, it will appear as **Object** on the model and be defined according to how the application defines the term, not how the business defines the term. As another example of reverse engineering, you might have as your starting point some type of physical data structure such as a database layout, or an XML or JSON document. For example, we can reverse engineer the following

JSON document to arrive at terms such as **Sport,** **Manufacturer,** and **Player:**

```
{
  "Sport":"Baseball",
  "Year":"1952",
  "Manufacturer":"Topps",
  "Number":311,
  "FirstName":"Mickey",
  "LastName":"Mantle",
  "PriceDate":"12/21/2018",
  "ConditionCode":"VG",
  "PostalCodeSold":"07834",
  "ConditionGradedBy":"PSA",
  "PriceUSD":38500,
  "ShippingUSD":4.95
}
```

5. **Operational or analytics?** This question ensures we choose the right type of BTM—either relational or dimensional. An operational initiative requires a relational BTM, and an analytics initiative requires a dimensional BTM.

6. **Who is our audience?** We need to know who will review our model (validator), and who will use our model going forward (users).

You were able to convince the executive team from Chapter 1 to postpone purchasing that software solution which would integrate business processes as "easy as baking a cookie", and are meeting with the team now to get answers to these six strategic questions.

1. What is our initiative?

Even though it was agreed that the first business process to integrate would be purchasing, the purchasing initiative may not yet have a clear scope, as we see in this dialog between you and the Chief Executive Officer, CEO, during this meeting after asking this first question.

> **CEO**: Eventually all of our processes will be centralized and consistent across our bakeries, yet our initial focus will be on purchasing.

> **You**: Understood. I visited that chic bakery nearby in that upscale neighborhood to try one of their cookies...I mean biscuits...and noticed they sell parfaits, smoothies, and artisan breads. I haven't seen these types of goods in our other bakeries—are these within the scope of our initiative as well?

> **CEO**: Hmm. I know about that bakery and part of their marketing and appeal with that neighborhood is that they purchase almost all of their ingredients locally. Let's make centralizing purchasing at least initially focused only on pastries.

> **You**: Done. How about pies? That bakery had lots of pies and I know our core business is cakes. Should we slice out pies as well?

> **CEO**: Slicing out pies, that's a good one. Ha, ha. Stick to your day job.

> **You**: Yes sir!

CEO: Pies are not so popular in our bakery chain yet—but they will become more popular as we are planning on including them in our franchising strategy. So make sure pies are within the scope of our purchasing initiative.

You: Good, I like pies. Since our focus is only on purchasing right now, is it ok to exclude the whole shipping and delivery process from suppliers?

CEO: Shipping and delivery are critical interactions with our suppliers, but let's wait and see how this first initiative goes. Get this first initiative right, and there's a promotion in it for you. Now get going and make this happen!

Free cookies are a nice perk, but landing that corner office—that would be something! Let's stop dreaming though and keep focused and move on to the next question with now knowing this refined purchasing scope.

2. Flexibility or simplicity?

CEO: I don't understand the question.

You: We need to determine whether to use generic terms or for lack of a better word, more concrete terms. Using generic terms such as organization instead of supplier and material instead of cookie allow us to accommodate future terms later. For example, if six months from now, you and your team decide to include smoothies within centralized purchasing, a smoothie would be just another example of a material that we would be able to easily accommodate.

CEO: Hmm. That sounds very appealing. That organization concept might work well later on when we think more in terms of other organizations such as franchisees, but for now we just have only one which is the supplier. However, the idea on material is an interesting one because there are lots of examples of materials such as cookies, cakes, pies, and so on.

You: Choosing a more flexible term such as material does not exclude showing the terms cookies and cakes. We can include material and use a technique called subtyping to include examples such as cookies and cakes and maybe eventually smoothies. Would this work?

Since the concept of Material seems very appealing, the executive team led by the CEO agree on flexibility. This means our model will contain some generic terms supplemented by subtyping.

3. Now or later?

CEO: After many years of letting each bakery define their own processes, I am the first to admit we have some big hurdles to overcome with centralizing any process, especially purchasing. The model you share with us needs to be aspirational—that is, show us where we need to be.

As we can see from our conversations on these first three questions, getting to the answers is rarely straightforward and easy. However, it is much cheaper and more Agile to ask them at the beginning of the initiative, instead of making assumptions early on and having to perform rework later, when changes will be time-consuming and expensive.

In Chapter 1, based on how quickly the executive team was being hypnotized by that software consultant, we were not sure whether they believed centralizing purchasing will be easy without realizing that each bakery speaks their own unique language, or that they knew there is a lack of a Common Business Language. Now we see that at least the CEO acknowledges a lack of a Common Business Language.

So based upon the CEO's remarks, we need to create a "later" view. That is, a holistic view showing how purchasing fits together, even if today that is not the case.

To reach this holistic view however, requires knowledge of the existing state. A data model of just a future view provides limited value unless we can show how to get there from our starting point (the "now" view). So we can choose a later view for our data model, but we will need to create a mapping to our existing environment.

4. Forward or reverse engineering?

Since we first need to understand how the business works before we can implement a centralized software solution, this is a forward engineering project and we will choose the forward engineering option. This means driven by requirements and therefore our terms will be business terms instead of application terms.

5. Operational or analytics?

Since this initiative is about centralizing the purchasing business process, which is operational, we will build a relational BTM and not dimensional.

6. Who is our audience?

That is, who is going to validate the model and who is going to use it going forward? The validators will be the executive team, and the users will be the software vendors who can use the model to ensure they are speaking the correct language with the executive team, and also to gauge how well their software applications would meet Chips Inc. needs.

Step 2: Identify and define the terms

Now that we have direction, we can work with the business experts to identify and define the terms within the scope of initiative.

Recall our definition of a term as a noun which represents a collection of business data and is considered both basic and critical to your audience for a particular initiative. A term can fit into one of six categories: who, what, when, where, why, or how. We can use these six categories to create a terms template for capturing the terms on our relational BTM.

Terms template

Who?	What?	When?	Where?	Why?	How?
1.	1.	1.	1.	1.	1.
2.	2.	2.	2.	2.	2.
3.	3.	3.	3.	3.	3.
4.	4.	4.	4.	4.	4.
5.	5.	5.	5.	5.	5.

This is a handy brainstorming tool. There is no significance to the numbers. That is, a term written next to #1 is not meant to be more important than a term written next to #2. In addition, you can have more than five terms in a given column, or in some cases no terms in a given column.

We met with the executive team and through a brainstorming session over lunch, completed the terms template on the facing page.

Chips Inc. purchasing terms

Who?	What?	When?	Where?	Why?	How?
Consumer Supplier	Semi-finished Material Ingredient Packaging Material Category Muffin Cupcake Pie Cake Cookie	Expiration Date Holiday Season	Bakery	Order Bill Shipment	Purchase Order Invoice Packing Slip Recipe

Notice that this is a brainstorming session, and there might be terms which appear on this template but do not appear on the purchasing BTM. Those terms that will be excluded fit into three categories:

- **Too detailed.** There are several concepts on this template that appear to be attributes and therefore will appear on the logical data model and not the BTM. For example, although **Expiration Date** and **Category** are important to Chips Inc., they are at a more detailed level than **Supplier** and **Purchase Order**.

- **Out of scope**. Brainstorming is a great way to test the scope of the initiative. Often terms come up that are added to the terms template which require additional discussions to determine whether they are in scope or not. For example, the CEO informed us that shipping and delivery are out of scope, yet terms such as **Packing Slip** and **Shipment** appear on this template. Even a critical term such as **Consumer** may not be critical for the purchasing process.

- **Transaction versus Document**. A document from the How column provides evidence that a transaction occurred from the Why column. Do we need to include a transaction term if everything about that transaction is provided by a document? For example, a **Purchase Order** document provides all of the content for the **Order** transaction. An **Invoice** document provides all of the content for the **Bill** transaction. A **Packing Slip** document provides all of the content for the **Shipment** transaction. Let's assume that the Chips Inc. executive team agrees to focus on documents rather than transactions for the scope of our initiative. Note that on many projects, I've experienced a user preference for focusing on documents due to documents being more tangible than transactions.

After taking a lunch break and revisiting the terms template, the executive team agreed to remove a number of terms from the template, shown here with strikethrough:

Chips Inc. purchasing terms (refined)

Who?	What?	When?	Where?	Why?	How?
~~Consumer~~ Supplier	Semi-finished Material Ingredient Packaging Material ~~Category~~ Muffin Cupcake Pie Cake Cookie	~~Expiration~~ ~~Date~~ ~~Holiday~~ ~~Season~~	Bakery	~~Order~~ ~~Bill~~ ~~Shipment~~	Purchase Order Invoice ~~Packing~~ ~~Slip~~ ~~Recipe~~

An additional important point here is that the mapping visual we discussed earlier might be needed to achieve a common language for some of these terms. In this example, because our audience is limited to the executive team, we most likely would not need a mapping visual. However, if we were meeting with several different bakeries and the purchasing experts across the bakeries had different perspectives for the same terms, then the mapping visual would become an invaluable stepping-stone towards completing this purchasing terms template.

Below is a spreadsheet that was produced after several sessions with the executive team discussing these terms in detail, containing terms, definitions, and questions.

Definitions and questions

Terms	Definitions	Questions
Supplier	The organization who provides materials to us.	The word "materials" is used. Is it limited to raw materials or can it be packaging materials and maybe even materials for sale, like cookies?
Semi-finished Material	A material that contains multiple ingredients and is usually input to a cookie or cake, such as melted chocolate or cookie dough.	What does the word "usually" mean in this context? "Usually" is a vague term that can include many exceptions to the norm. Are there exceptions? Can you ever sell a semi-finished material, such as cookie dough?
Ingredient	Something that, from the perspective of the bakery purchaser, cannot be broken down into smaller pieces, such as sugar or milk.	Can we use the word "material" instead of "something"? Since it is "from the perspective of the bakery purchaser," can a material be considered an ingredient by one purchaser but not by another?

Terms	Definitions	Questions
Packaging Material	A covering for the material that has been purchased, such as a box for a cake or bag for a cupcake.	Is packaging material limited to protecting the consumer's purchase, or can it include packaging on items the bakery purchases, such as packaging for sugar?
Muffin	A large cupcake without frosting.	By putting frosting on a muffin, does it become a cupcake? If yes, is a muffin a semi-finished material for a cupcake?
Cupcake	A muffin with frosting.	Muffin and cupcake have circular definitions. That is, each definition defines its term using the other term.
Pie	Some type of fruit encased in a pastry shell.	Not clear on the distinction yet between pie and cake.
Cake	A block of solid substance made from or based on a mixture of flour and sugar and eggs.	This sounds like it was copied from an online dictionary. How does Chips Inc. define a cake?
Cookie	Also known as a biscuit, a cookie is a small round sweet pastry.	This definition does not exclude muffins or cupcakes. How does a cookie differ from a muffin or cupcake?
Bakery	One of our locations today and that in the future could be a franchise location.	Why is it important to distinguish one of our bakeries from one that has been franchised?
Purchase Order	The confirmation that we have successfully placed an order.	How do you know if an order was not placed successfully?
Invoice	A document confirming we have been billed for a purchase.	Can an invoice be for more than one purchase order? Or is there always a one-to-one relationship between a purchase order and invoice?

Note that I included lots of questions—not to answer them for this initiative but instead to illustrate the three benefits of raising questions:

- **Become known as the detective.** Become comfortable with the level of detective work needed to arrive at a precise set of terms. Look for holes in the definition where ambiguity can sneak in, and ask questions the answers to which will remove this ambiguity and make the definition precise. Consider the question "Can an invoice be for more than one purchase order?" The answer to this question will refine how Chips Inc. views invoices, purchase orders, and their relationship.

- **Uncover hidden terms.** Often the answers to questions lead to more terms on our BTM - terms that we might have missed otherwise. For example, better understanding the relationship between **Purchase Order** and **Invoice** might lead to more terms on our BTM which handle account reconciliation.

- **Better now than later.** The resulting BTM offers a lot of value yet the process of getting to that final model is also valuable. Debates and questions challenge people and make them rethink and in some cases defend their perspectives. If questions are not raised and answered during the process of building the BTM, the questions will be raised and need to be addressed later on in the lifecycle of the initiative, often in the form of data and process surprises, when changes are time-consuming and expensive. Even simple questions like "How do you know if an order was not placed successfully?" can lead to a heathy debate resulting in a more precise BTM.

Here is our model after identifying and defining the terms:

Just our terms

Supplier	Muffin	Cookie
Semi-finished	Cupcake	Bakery
Ingredient	Pie	Purchase Order
Packaging Material	Cake	Invoice

Before we start looking at the relationships, I like to group common terms together for better comprehension, as shown on the model on the next page.

Common terms grouped together

	Supplier	
Cookie	Bakery	
		Purchase Order
Muffin		Invoice
Pie		
Cake	Ingredient	
Cupcake	Semi-finished	Packaging Material

Cookie, **Muffin**, **Pie**, **Cake**, and **Cupcake** are all items that are available for sale in the bakery. We need to ask what term would encompass all of these. That is, what would be the supertype of these five terms? Let's say after a brief debate with the executive team, the term **Finished Material** is chosen. This term is chosen to be consistent with **Semi-finished Material** (shortened to **Semi-finished**) and **Packaging Material**.

Ingredient and **Semi-finished** also seem to be highly-related, as both are raw materials for a **Finished Material**. After some discussion with the business, the term **Raw Material** is accepted as a supertype for **Ingredient** and **Semi-Finished Material**.

The following is our model with supertypes added.

Supertypes added

Finished Material
- Cookie
- Muffin
- Pie
- Cake
- Cupcake

Supplier

Bakery

Purchase Order

Invoice

Raw Material
- Ingredient
- Semi-finished

Packaging Material

What else do you notice about this model?

Finished Material, Raw Material, and **Packaging Material** seem like they are related as well. So why can't we do this?

Material as a supertype?

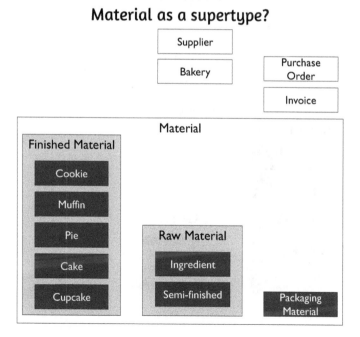

Here we have the supertype **Material** and the subtypes **Finished Material**, **Raw Material**, and **Packaging Material**. Is this model correct?

Subtyping is useful in showing examples of the supertype. For example, a **Cookie** is an example of a **Finished Material**. However, is a **Finished Material** an example of a **Material**?

A **Finished Material** is not an example of a **Material**, but instead a role of the **Material**. That is a **Material** can play the roles of **Finished Material**, **Raw Material**, and **Packaging Material**.

Material Role added

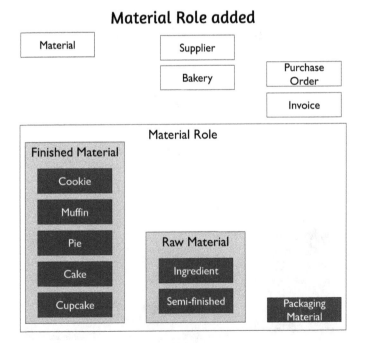

For example, the **Material** cookie dough can play the role of a **Semi-finished Material** for chocolate chip cookies and the role of a **Finished Material** if Chips Inc. starts selling cookie dough in their bakeries.

The role concept in general fits nicely with categorizing your terms into Who, What, When, Where, Why, and How, as each of these categories has a corresponding role. A Who such as **Person** can play the roles of **Employee** or **Student**. A What such as **Material** can play the roles of **Raw Material** or **Finished Product** depending on whether it is sold to a consumer. A When such as **Time** can play the roles of **Arrival Time** or **Departure Time** for an airline. A Where such as **Address** can play the roles of **Billing Address** or **Shipping Address** for a particular **Order**. A Why such as **Feedback** can play the roles of **Compliment** or **Complaint**. A How such as **Document** can play the roles of **Author Agreement** or **Reseller Agreement**.

Material and **Material Role** have a relationship, which we'll create in the next section!

Step 3: Capture the relationships

The relationships of a relational BTM represent business rules. Recall the Participation and Existence questions that need to be answered to precisely display the business rules for each relationship. Participation questions determine whether there is a one or a many symbol on the relationship line next to each term. Existence questions determine whether there is a zero (may) or one (must) symbol on the relationship line next to either term.

So returning to **Material** and **Material Role**, here are the four questions along with answers:

Question	Yes	No
Can a Material play more than one Material Role?	✓	
Can a Material Role be played by more than one Material?		✓
Can a Material exist without a Material Role?	✓	
Can a Material Role exist without a Material?		✓

The answers to these questions lead to the model on the facing page.

The relationship between Material and Material role is read as:

- Each **Material** may play many **Material Roles**.
- Each **Material Role** must be played by one **Material**.

Material and Material Role connected

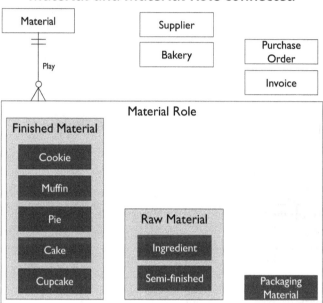

Working with the executive team, we have identified these five additional relationships on the model:

- **Bakery** and **Material Role**
- **Supplier** and **Purchase Order**
- **Material Role** and **Purchase Order**
- **Supplier** and **Invoice**
- **Material Role** and **Invoice**

The facing page contains answers to the Participation and Existence questions for each of these five relationships.

Question	Yes	No
Can a Bakery use more than one Material Role?	✓	
Can a Material Role be used by more than one Bakery?	✓	
Can a Bakery exist without a Material Role?	✓	
Can a Material Role exist without a Bakery?	✓	
Can a Supplier receive more than one Purchase Order?	✓	
Can a Purchase Order be received by more than one Supplier?		✓
Can a Supplier exist without a Purchase Order?	✓	
Can a Purchase Order exist without a Supplier?		✓
Can a Material Role appear on more than one Purchase Order?	✓	
Can a Purchase Order reference more than one Material Role?	✓	
Can a Material Role exist without a Purchase Order?	✓	
Can a Purchase Order exist without a Material Role?		✓
Can a Supplier create more than one Invoice?	✓	
Can an Invoice be created by more than one Supplier?		✓
Can a Supplier exist without an Invoice?	✓	
Can an Invoice exist without a Supplier?		✓
Can a Material Role appear on more than one Invoice?	✓	
Can an Invoice reference more than one Material Role?	✓	
Can a Material Role exist without an Invoice?	✓	
Can an Invoice exist without a Material Role?		✓

After translating the answers to each of these questions into the model, we have the following model.

Purchasing BTM

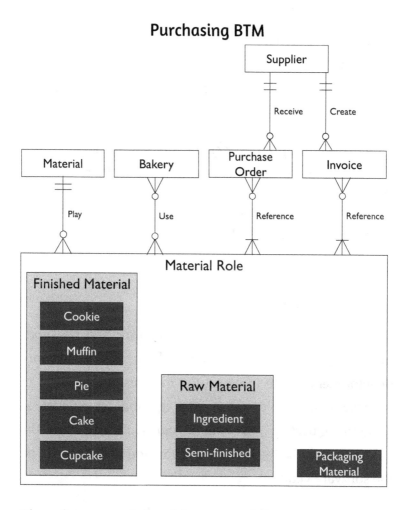

These five new relationships are read as:

- Each **Bakery** may use many **Material Roles**.
- Each **Material Role** may be used by many **Bakeries**.

- Each **Supplier** may receive many **Purchase Orders**.
- Each **Purchase Order** must be received by one **Supplier**.

- Each **Purchase Order** must reference many **Material Roles**.
- Each **Material Role** may appear on many **Purchase Orders**.

- Each **Supplier** may create many **Invoices**.
- Each **Invoice** must be created by one **Supplier**.

- Each **Invoice** must reference many **Material Roles**.
- Each **Material Role** may appear on many **Invoices**.

Step 4: Determine the visual

Someone will need to review your work and use your model as input for future deliverables such as software development, so deciding on the most useful visual is an important step. We know after getting an answer to Strategic Question #4, *Who is our audience?*, that the validators will be the executive team, and the users will be the software vendors.

There are many different ways of displaying the BTM. Factors include the technical competence of the audience and the existing tools environment. Ideally, we can use the same notation we have been using throughout the book:

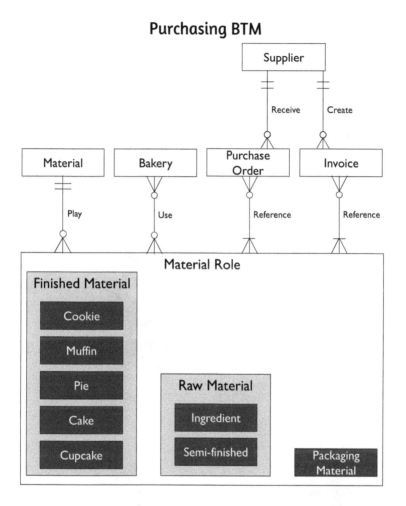

Purchasing BTM

However, it would be helpful to know which data modeling notations and data modeling tools are currently being used within the organization. If the audience is familiar with a particular data modeling notation—such as Information Engineering (IE), which we have been using throughout this book—that is the notation we should use. If the audience is familiar with a particular data modeling tool, such as IDERA's ER/Studio, erwin DM, Hackolade, and that data modeling tool uses a different notation, we should use that tool with that notation to create the BTM.

Sometimes at the business terms level, the validators and users may not want to see the BTM in any data modeling notation. In these situations, be creative with displaying the model. For example, the following is a business sketch that can be used instead of Information Engineering.

Purchasing business sketch

Step 5: Review and confirm

Previously we identified the person or group responsible for validating the model. Now we need to show them the model and make sure it is correct. Often at this stage, after reviewing the model we go back and make some changes and then show them the model again. This iterative cycle continues until the model is agreed upon by the validator and approved—with this purchasing BTM we would seek approval from the executive team.

Dimensional

Now let's build a dimensional BTM for an analytics initiative following the five steps shown on the next page.

Steps to create a BTM

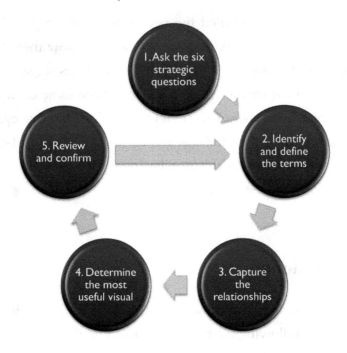

Step 1: Ask the six strategic questions

Six strategic questions

1	What is our initiative?
2	Flexibility or simplicity?
3	Now or later?
4	Forward or reverse engineering?
5	Operational or analytical?
6	Who is our audience?

Chips Inc. employs an accountant who is very knowledgeable on the bakery's finances. Let's meet with her and ask the six questions for this analytics initiative.

1. What is our initiative?

This question ensures we know enough about this analytics initiative to determine the scope. Knowing the scope allows us to decide which terms should appear on the initiative's BTM. The following is our conversation with the accountant after asking this question.

> **Accountant**: Every year I produce store-level and corporate-level tax returns. I am stuck in the financial details, and lack knowledge of how we are doing overall. Knowing how we are doing will set a benchmark for how well the Franchise program is doing and also how much we are saving from centralizing our business processes.

> **You**: Ok, got it. Tell me more—how would we know how well we are doing?

> **Accountant**: We would look at our profit.

> **You**: How do you determine profit?

> **Accountant**: Sales minus costs. So we need to see sales and costs too. Knowing the cost for example, will tell us the success or failure of centralizing purchasing and payroll.

> **You**: Ok, and by what level of detail would it be useful to view profit, sales, and costs?

Accountant: I need to know for each bakery and across all bakeries, by date, quarter, and year, and using the correct term from that successful Purchasing BTM, by finished material.

You: Great to hear that the Common Business Language created by the Purchasing BTM is starting to stick. Ok, I get the levels of detail needed. So you don't want to see the measures at a lower level than date, such as whether sales are better before lunch or after lunch, or at a higher level than date such as by day of week?

Accountant: Good point. I don't need to see them at a lower level than date, but knowing the day of week and also maybe how these measurements vary by holiday, such as for Christmas or Halloween, would be very useful.

You: Sounds good. Ok, let me get these ideas down and I'm sure I'll have more questions for you. Thanks for your time!

So we know that our scope is going to be the revenue process because we are measuring bakery success in terms of sales, cost, and profit.

2. Flexibility or simplicity?

This question ensures we introduce generic terms only if there is a need for flexibility. Although generic terms allow us to accommodate new types of terms that we do not know about today, generic terms also increase model vagueness and therefore almost 100% of the time we choose simplicity over flexibility for analytics. This is because the purpose of analytics is to easily answer quantitative questions. Which is an easier question to answer?

1. How many cookies did we sell? (Simple)
2. How many things did we sell where the thing type is cookie? (Flexible)

Definitely the first one!

We asked the accountant this question just to make sure, and she confirmed that simplicity is the priority.

I say almost 100% of the time we choose simplicity and not always 100% because there are always exceptions in the world of data management. I once worked on an analytics application for a branch of the federal government for example, and each of the states had their own unique requirements. Rather than create 50 different analytics apps, we chose flexibility over simplicity for our model, allowing each state to add their unique requirements without having to restructure or recode the application.

3. Now or later?

For the Purchasing Initiative, we chose "later" because we needed to capture a centralized purchasing environment which does not exist today for Chips Inc. For our revenue BTM, we also would like to model terms that do not exist today. The accountant needs varying and more summarized ways of viewing costs, sales, and profit. Therefore, we need to take a "later" perspective with this BTM as well.

4. Forward or reverse engineering?

Similar to the Chips Inc. relational BTM, we are driving this application from the accountant's requirements and not from an existing application. So this too is a forward engineering project.

5. Operational or analytics?

Since this initiative requires performing analytics, such as viewing profit at a date level and then summing up to a quarter level, we will build a dimensional BTM and not relational.

6. Who is our audience?

The accountant will validate our model and most likely the executive team will use our model going forward. It's possible that the marketing and sales team would also benefit from the model, as well as the vendor who will provide or develop the revenue analytics application.

Step 2: Identify and define the terms

Now that we have direction, we can work with the accountant to identify the terms within the scope of the initiative and come up with an agreed-upon definition for each term. Identifying and defining the terms from a dimensional perspective involves defining the quantitative questions that the analytics solution will eventually answer. For example, imagine that after our next meeting with the accountant, you have captured these quantitative questions:

1. What are our costs, sales, and profit by bakery and across all bakeries, for a particular date, quarter, and year, and for one or more finished materials?

2. What are our costs, sales, and profit by bakery and across all bakeries, for a particular day of the week and for one or more finished materials?

3. What are our costs, sales, and profit by bakery and across all bakeries, for a particular holiday and for one or more finished materials?

Step 3: Capture the relationships

For dimensional, we need to take the business questions we identified in the prior step and then create a measure matrix.

A measure matrix is a spreadsheet where measures from the business questions, such as cost and profit, become columns, and dimensional levels from each business question, such as date and quarter, become rows. The purpose of a measure matrix is to efficiently scope analytics solutions.

We can plot hundreds of business questions on a measure matrix, and then observe similarities between questions from different departments. We can then group similar measures and dimensional levels together into proposed analytics initiatives, making the measure matrix a fantastic tool for translating and scoping business questions into projects.

So for example, Chips Inc. might have over 100 quantitative questions that management would like answered, and all of these questions can be plotted on a measure matrix. Once the questions are plotted, we can group them into initiatives, such as like this:

Measure matrix very high level

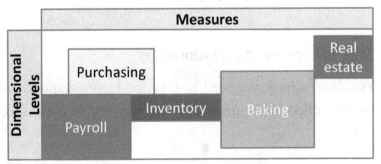

There might have been 20 purchasing-related questions that become grouped into a purchasing analytics application, 15 payroll-related questions grouped into a payroll reporting system, and so on.

We did not collect hundreds of business questions with anticipation of using the measure matrix to scope many different initiatives for Chips Inc. Instead, we collected only three questions from the accountant, so our measure matrix will be for only one initiative, revenue analytics.

Let's plot our three questions on a measure matrix. The numbers in the measure matrix refer back to the previous three question numbers.

Revenue measure matrix

	Costs	Sales	Profit
Date	1	1	1
Quarter	1	1	1
Year	1	1	1
Day of Week	2	2	2
Holiday	3	3	3
Bakery	1,2,3	1,2,3	1,2,3
Finished Material	1,2,3	1,2,3	1,2,3

Step 4: Determine the most useful visual

The accountant is our validator and therefore we need to find out what type of visual she would find most beneficial. In addition, we need to ensure the users such as the executive team have a useful visual. We can use pictures or photos to visualize the dimensional BTM, but often I find the Axis Technique is ideal.

Axis technique

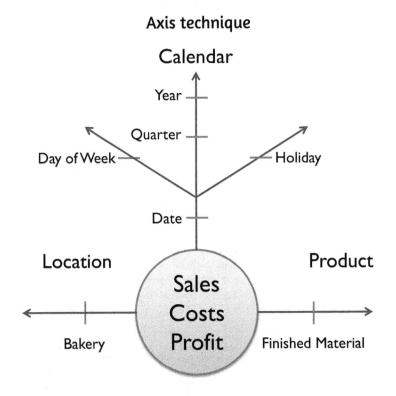

The Axis Technique is when you put measure names such as **Sales**, **Costs**, and **Profit**, or the business process name, such as **Revenue**, in the center circle—with each axis representing a dimension. The notches on each axis represent the levels of granularity needed for the measures. We need to see **Sales**, **Costs**, and **Profit** by **Bakery**, **Date**, and **Finished Material**. Sometimes instead of **Date** we might want to see these three measurements at the higher levels of **Quarter**, **Year**, **Day of Week** or **Holiday**.

An important benefit of the Axis Technique, besides being extremely intuitive, is that we can show complex navigation paths very easily. We can view **Sales** for the **Bakery** A for the **Finished Material** chocolate chip cookies on the **Date** February 1, 2020, for example, and then for this same **Bakery** and **Finished Material**, view **Sales** for the **Quarter** Q12020 or the **Year** 2020. We can also choose a different navigation path and see **Sales** by the **Day of Week** Monday or the **Holiday** Valentine's Day.

Day of Week and **Holiday** do not have a correlation with each other or with **Quarter**. For example, October 31, 2019 captures the **Holiday** Halloween and the **Day of Week** Thursday. October 31, 2018 however, captures the **Holiday** Halloween and the **Day of Week** Wednesday. In addition, November 28, 2019 captures the **Holiday** Thanksgiving and the **Day of Week** Thursday.

Step 5: Review and confirm

We need to review our BTM with the validator, our accountant, to make sure it is correct. Often at this stage, after reviewing the model we go back and make some changes and then meet to review the model again. This iterative cycle continues until the model is approved.

Maintain

Our organizations change over time and therefore the BTMs need to sometimes change as well. Luckily, since BTMs contain business terms and not detailed data structures, they don't change often. But when an organization makes large changes, such as buying a company, selling a company, getting in to a new business line or divesting of a business line—these types of changes can impact our models.

If we don't maintain the models, they lose value very quickly. As soon as a user for the model notices something no longer current on a BTM, there is a good chance that the user will never trust or use that BTM again.

Make sure there is a role or group responsible for maintaining BTMs within your organization.

Takeaways

Before you begin any project, there are six strategic questions that must be asked (Step 1). These questions are a prerequisite to the success of any initiative because they ensure we choose the right terms for our BTM. Next, identify all terms within the scope of the initiative (Step 2). Make sure each term is clearly and completely defined. Then determine how these terms are related to each other (Step 3). Often, you will need to go back to Step 2 at this point, because in capturing relationships you may come up with new terms. Next, determine the most beneficial visual for your audience (Step 4). Consider the visual that would resonate best with those that will need to review and use your BTM. As a final step, seek approval of your BTM (Step 5). Often at this point there are additional changes to the model, and we cycle through these steps until the model is accepted.

CHAPTER 5

Practice

And now, let's have some fun!

In this chapter I will build two BTMs, one relational for an operational initiative and one dimensional for an analytics initiative. You will have an opportunity to build your own relational and dimensional BTMs as we progress through each of the five steps.

Relational

If the goal of the initiative is to capture how a business process works, in anticipation of introducing, replacing, integrating, or customizing an operational application, then the rules governing the terms are very important to understand and capture, and therefore a relational BTM is needed. Let's go through the five steps to build a relational BTM.

Steps to create a BTM

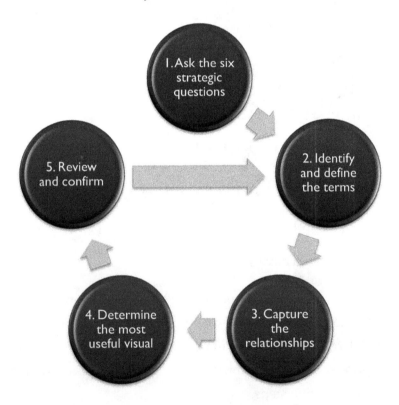

Step 1: Ask the six strategic questions

Six strategic questions

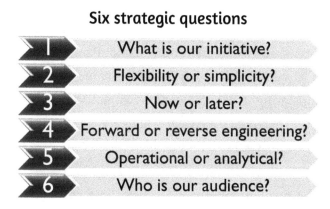

1. What is our initiative?
2. Flexibility or simplicity?
3. Now or later?
4. Forward or reverse engineering?
5. Operational or analytical?
6. Who is our audience?

1. What is our initiative?

This question ensures we know enough about the initiative to determine the scope. Knowing the scope allows us to decide which terms should appear on the initiative's BTM.

I ran our first Data Modeling Zone conference in 2012. Visit https://datamodelingzone.com/ to learn more about future conferences, as there are sessions not only on BTMs but also on logical and physical data modeling. Maybe you can present a case study of your success with using the BTM!

Today there are three conferences a year—one in the US that I continue to organize and ones in Europe and Australia which I co-organize. I manage attendees using the same process and tools from 2012 however, with

Microsoft Excel being my primary tool. Don't be so surprised: most organizations today still run on Excel!

With an environment that is getting more and more complex due to registration customization, such as someone registering for the full event versus someone else just registering for a pre-conference tutorial, as well as multiple personal privacy laws that vary across regions—the GDPR in Europe, The Privacy Act in Australia, and various privacy acts around the United States—I need to better understand and consolidate our attendee data and therefore better understand the terms within the attendee arena.

Once I better understand the attendee arena, I can intelligently evaluate software solutions built for managing attendees.

Let's call this project the *Attendee Initiative*. Remember the best way to learn is to practice, so grab a paper and pencil and follow along!

What is your initiative?

This Attendee Initiative will require capturing how the attendee registration and check-in processes work. Registration is when someone signs up to attend the Data Modeling Zone conference, and check-in is when they arrive at the conference and pick up their conference badge. The scope of my initiative is the attendee.

2. Flexibility or simplicity?

This question ensures we introduce generic terms only if there is a need for flexibility. Generic terms allow us to accommodate new types of terms that are currently unknown or out of scope. For example, choosing **Person** as a more generic term than **Attendee** would allow us to accommodate additional types of people such as staff and speakers.

Did you choose flexibility or simplicity for your initiative?

Do I need flexibility? If our goal is to better understand the attendee, why not focus on attendees and let **Attendee** be our term instead of **Person**? Let's, at least initially, choose simplicity and create the term **Attendee**. Note that sometimes our perspective changes from simplicity to flexibility as we start to learn more about the initiative. You might see that here. (Spoiler-alert!)

3. Now or later?

This question ensures we have chosen the correct time perspective for our BTM. If we are intent on capturing how business processes work today, then we need to make sure our model reflects a current perspective (now). If we are intent on capturing how business processes work at some point from now, then we need a future perspective (later).

Did you choose a now or later perspective for your initiative?

I have outgrown our disparate Excel-driven attendee registration and check-in processes and need more consolidated processes for managing attendees. A consolidated attendee perspective does not exist today, requiring me to choose the "later" view. This means that I will need a mapping from my current disparate Excel-driven environment to the new more holistic environment.

Attendee Initiative mapping from now to later

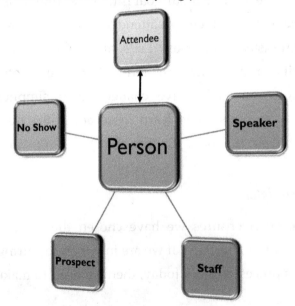

Consider the above mapping a preview for what might be coming as we progress through the five steps. It is possible that today I see the world in terms of narrow roles such as **Attendee** and **Speaker**. From the later perspective, I might recognize **Attendee** and **Speaker** as roles a **Person** can play. Maps such as the above help us migrate from a now to later perspective. Returning to the strategic question on flexibility or simplicity, maybe we should aim more for flexibility and introduce **Person**.

4. Forward or reverse engineering?

This question ensures we are selecting the most appropriate "language" for the BTM. If the initiative is being driven by business requirements, then it is a forward engineering effort and we choose a business language. If the initiative is being driven by an application, then it is a reverse engineering effort and we choose an application language.

Did you choose forward or reverse engineering for your initiative?

Since I first need to understand the business language within the attendee environment before we introduce some type of software solution, this is a forward engineering project and I will choose the forward engineering option. This means driven by requirements and therefore my terms will be business terms and not application terms.

5. Operational or analytics?

This question ensures we choose the right type of BTM—either relational for operational or dimensional for analytics. I need to focus on the rules within the attendee environment, and therefore this will be operational and I will build a relational BTM. For your first model, make sure you chose relational as well.

6. Who is our audience?

We need to know who will review our model (validator), and who will use our model going forward (users). The reason for this question is to ensure we build the right type of visual. If, for example, the validator and users are comfortable with the notation we have learned in this book, then that will be the notation we use. Otherwise, we might need to get creative and find a different way to present the BTM, such as the example we saw in the last chapter.

Who are the validators and users for your initiative?

My colleagues who help me organize the conferences will be the validators. They will be the ones who tell me if the model is correct or needs changes. Software vendors who might have a solution I can use, will be the users of the model. The vendors can study my BTM and determine whether they have a solution that would meet my needs.

Step 2: Identify and define the terms

Now that we have direction, we can work with the business experts to identify the terms within the scope of the application and come up with an agreed-upon definition for each term. A term can fit into one of six categories: who, what, when, where, why, or how. We can use these six categories to create a terms template for capturing the terms on our relational BTM.

Complete this terms template for your initiative. Create a mapping visual as illustrated in the last chapter if your audience uses different terms for the same thing.

Your initiative terms template

Who?	What?	When?	Where?	Why?	How?
1.	1.	1.	1.	1.	1.
2.	2.	2.	2.	2.	2.
3.	3.	3.	3.	3.	3.
4.	4.	4.	4.	4.	4.
5.	5.	5.	5.	5.	5.

And here is the terms template completed for my initiative:

Attendee initiative terms

Who?	What?	When?	Where?	Why?	How?
Attendee	Conference		Venue	Registration	Contact Mechanism
Speaker	Conference Option			Promotion	
Prospect				Payment	
No Show					

There are a couple of observations we can make based upon this template:

- **Broader than Attendee**. We can see four terms in the Who column, of which **Attendee** is just one type of person. Remember our simplicity over flexibility choice discussed earlier? These four terms are roles that a **Person** can play. Building on the mapping discussion a few pages back, we most likely will opt for flexibility, as what if **Staff** becomes within scope in the near future? Expect **Person** and **Person Role** terms on my BTM. In fact, we might change the name of the initiative from the Attendee Initiative to the Person Initiative.

- **No When terms**. There are no terms in the When column. This can either mean that we missed terms, or that there really are no calendar- or time-based terms as part of this initiative.

- **Why and How are similar. Registration, Promotion,** and **Payment** can be documents in the How column just as easy as being events in the Why column. For example, there could be a registration event after one completes the action of registering for Data Modeling Zone. There also could be a registration document emailed to that person confirming their registration.

Below is a spreadsheet that was produced after several discussions with my conference team, containing initial terms, definitions, and outstanding questions.

Definitions and questions

Terms	Definitions	Questions
Attendee	A person who has registered to attend a Data Modeling Zone conference. They may have paid or been given a discounted or free pass (known as a beta pass) to the conference. Speakers and staff are not considered attendees.	Is it important to distinguish a paid attendee from an attendee that attends for free? If someone pays and then cancels, are they still considered an attendee? Is staff within the scope of the initiative?

Terms	Definitions	Questions
Speaker	A person who has been accepted to present one or more sessions at a Data Modeling Zone conference.	If someone is scheduled to speak, and they cancel, are they still considered a speaker? Is it important to know about those speakers who cancel? Are there different types of speakers, such as those that deliver keynotes, sit on panels, or facilitate sessions?
Prospect	A person who is a good candidate to attend a Data Modeling Zone conference.	Could an attendee at one Data Modeling Zone conference become a prospect for another Data Modeling Zone conference? When does a previous attendee become a prospect? Are there different types of prospects based on their potential of attendance?
No Show	An attendee or speaker who does not show up for the conference.	If an attendee shows up on Monday for the conference, but not Tuesday, are they considered a no show? If someone attends for just part of a day, such as skipping the afternoon sessions, would this be considered a no show?
Conference	A planned event and venue for a Data Modeling Zone conference.	How does an event differ from a conference?

Terms	Definitions	Questions
Conference Option	A different registration option for the conference.	Examples would be useful in this definition.
Venue	A hotel or similar type of building where the conference is held.	Is it important to distinguish a hotel from a "similar type of building"?
Registration	An agreement between an attendee and us that they will be attending one of our conferences for a particular conference option.	At what point does a prospect become an attendee? Is it when they click the Register button after filling in their information, or when they pay for the conference?
Promotion	A discount that is being offered as an incentive for someone to register for a conference. Examples include early bird discounts and discounts for media representatives.	Should media representative be another type of attendee?
Payment	The amount of money that a person pays to become an attendee.	What types of payment details are we storing for each attendee based on the type of payment? For example, are credit card numbers being stored for those that pay with credit cards?
Contact Mechanism	The different ways we can contact a person, such as by phone or email.	Are there different ways to contact a person based on that person's roles?

> *Fill in a similar spreadsheet containing definitions and questions for your initiative.*

We will not invest space here answering the above questions and in seeing how these answers impact our model. However, recall from our discussion in the last chapter about the value of questions. We might for example, when learning the answers to the **Attendee** questions, learn that **Staff** is truly within the scope of the initiative and will need to be added to the table above and as a term on our model.

Here are the terms grouped together by the column they appeared in on our terms template:

Common terms grouped together

Attendee	Conference	Registration
Speaker	Conference Option	Promotion
Prospect		Payment
No Show		
	Venue	
		Contact Mechanism

Grouping this way makes it easy to identify supertypes. Here we identify the **Person Role** and **Person Event** supertypes.

Attendee, Speaker, Prospect and **No Show** are not people, but instead roles that a **Person** can play. Bob is a **Person** playing the role of a **Prospect** until he registers. Now he is playing the role of an **Attendee**. He might also be a **Speaker**, and if he does not show up for the conference he will play the role of a **No Show**. So I separated the **Person** from the roles the **Person** plays.

Supertypes added

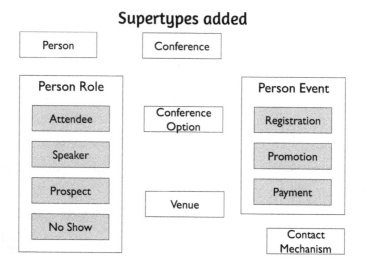

Reading the two subtyping structures, we have:

- Each **Person Role** may be an **Attendee, Speaker, Prospect** or **No Show**.
- **Attendee** is a **Person Role**.

- **Speaker** is a **Person Role**.
- **Prospect** is a **Person Role**.
- **No Show** is a **Person Role**.

- Each **Person Event** may be a **Registration, Promotion,** or **Payment.**
- **Registration** is a **Person Event.**
- **Promotion** is a **Person Event.**
- **Payment** is a **Person Event.**

Are there opportunities to introduce subtyping or roles in your BTM?

Step 3: Capture the relationships

Relational BTM relationships represent business rules. Recall the Participation and Existence questions that need to be answered to precisely display the business rules for each relationship. Participation questions determine whether there is a one or a many symbol on the relationship line next to each term. Existence questions determine whether there is a zero (may) or one (must) symbol on the relationship line next to either term.

While discussing terms and their meanings, my team and I identified these six relationships:

- **Person** and **Person Role**
- **Person Role and Person Event**

- **Venue** and **Conference**
- **Conference and Conference Option**
- **Conference Option and Person Event**
- **Person Role and Contact Mechanism**

I now need to capture the four questions for each relationship. In the last chapter, I shared with you two question templates, one with only the questions and then one with the answers as well. To save a page, I am just going to share with you one template with answers.

Question	Yes	No
Can a Person play more than one Person Role?	✓	
Can a Person Role be played by more than one Person?		✓
Can a Person exist without a Person Role?	✓	
Can a Person Role exist without a Person?		✓
Can a Person Role initiate more than one Person Event?	✓	
Can a Person Event be initiated by more than one Person Role?		✓
Can a Person Role exist without a Person Event?	✓	
Can a Person Event exist without a Person Role?		✓
Can a Venue be the location for more than one Conference?	✓	
Can a Conference be located at more than one Venue?		✓
Can a Venue exist without a Conference?	✓	
Can a Conference exist without a Venue?		✓

Question	Yes	No
Can a Conference offer more than one Conference Option?	✓	
Can a Conference Option be offered at more than one Conference?		✓
Can a Conference exist without a Conference Option?	✓	
Can a Conference Option exist without a Conference?		✓
Can a Conference Option include more than one Person Event?	✓	
Can a Person Event be included in more than one Conference Option?		✓
Can a Conference Option exist without a Person Event?	✓	
Can a Person Event exist without a Conference Option?		✓
Can a Person Role be reached by more than one Contact Mechanism?	✓	
Can a Contact Mechanism reach more than one Person Role?		✓
Can a Person Role exist without a Contact Mechanism`?	✓	
Can a Contact Mechanism exist without a Person Role?		✓

Identify the relationships for your initiative and complete a template such as the one above to structure the four questions for each relationship. Find a knowledgeable resource and have them answer each of the questions in your spreadsheet.

The answers to these questions led to the following model.

Person Initiative BTM

Create the BTM based on the answers to your questions.

The new relationships are read as:

- Each **Venue** may be the location for many **Conferences**.
- Each **Conference** must be located at one **Venue**.

- Each **Conference** may offer many **Conference Options**.
- Each **Conference Option** must be offered at one **Conference**.

- Each **Conference Option** may include many **Person Events**.
- Each **Person Event** must be included in one **Conference Option**.

- Each **Person** may play many **Person Roles**.
- Each **Person Role** must be played by one **Person**.

- Each **Person Role** may initiate many **Person Events**.
- Each **Person Event** must be initiated by one **Person Role**.

- Each **Person Role** may be reached by many **Contact Mechanisms**.
- Each **Contact Mechanism** must reach one **Person Role**.

Articulate the relationships like I did above for each relationship on your model.

Step 4: Determine the visual

In terms of the visual, I am going to use the symbols we have learned in this book, and the model above becomes my final model.

Which type of visual did you choose for your initiative?

Think of your validator and users when choosing the type of visual.

A very important benefit to using symbols such as those on the model above, is that these same symbols are frequently used on more detailed logical and physical data models. For example, this subset of my BTM:

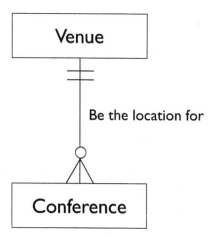

Might look like this on a logical data model:

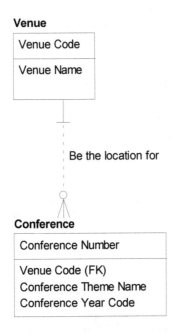

Venue

Venue Code
Venue Name

Be the location for

Conference

Conference Number
Venue Code (FK) Conference Theme Name Conference Year Code

Notice that although there is additional detail on this model, you can read the relationship the same way as on the BTM.

Step 5: Review and confirm

I meet with my team and we sign off on the model.

Part of this review process is to address any outstanding questions and often the answers can lead to more changes to our model and improvements to our definitions.

Dimensional

If the goal of the initiative is to capture how well a business process is performing in anticipation of introducing, replacing, integrating, or customizing an analytical application, then quantitative questions are very important to identify and capture. Let's go through the five steps to building a BTM, this time for a dimensional BTM.

Steps to create a BTM

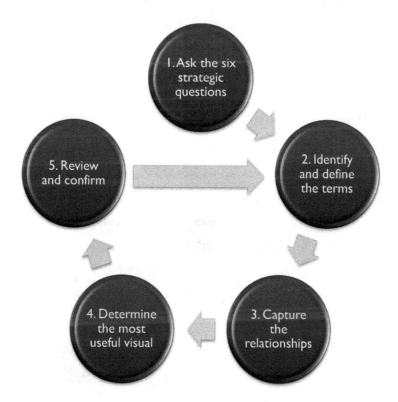

Step 1: Ask the six strategic questions

Ask yourself these six questions for your dimensional BTM and then read below to see the answers for my analytics initiative.

Six strategic questions

1	**What is our initiative?**
2	**Flexibility or simplicity?**
3	**Now or later?**
4	**Forward or reverse engineering?**
5	**Operational or analytical?**
6	**Who is our audience?**

1. What is our initiative?

We have sponsors who pay money to exhibit and in some cases speak at our conferences. My *Sponsor Initiative* will allow me to analyze each sponsor's involvement in each conference, along with how much revenue we have collected from each sponsor. I can then award sponsors who have shown greater loyalty to our conferences by giving them more visible exhibitor locations and more prominent speaking slots.

We will analyze how well sponsorships are doing for each conference, and therefore it is an analytics project requiring a dimensional BTM. Once we understand the analytics required of the Sponsor Initiative, I will hire a developer to build an analytics tool for us to use.

What is your initiative?

My Sponsor Initiative focuses on sponsors and their investments in our conferences over time.

2. Flexibility or simplicity?

As mentioned earlier, most dimensional BTMs are simple rather than flexible because it is easier to understand analytics when using simple terms that the business uses as opposed to more generic terms that are harder to grasp such as **Person** or **Party**. If I choose flexibility, this will mean that an attendee might be called a **Person** or a **Party**. This will accommodate other types of people or parties such as company employees and sponsors.

Did you choose flexibility or simplicity for your initiative?

But do I need flexibility? If our goal is to better understand the sponsor, shouldn't we focus on sponsor and let **Sponsor** be our term instead of **Party**?

I think so and therefore we will choose simplicity.

3. Now or later?

This question ensures we have chosen the correct time perspective for our BTM.

Did you choose a now or later perspective for your initiative?

I need to know about our current sponsor environment. Therefore I will choose the "now" view.

4. Forward or reverse engineering?

This question ensures we are selecting the most appropriate "language" for the BTM.

Did you choose forward or reverse engineering for your initiative?

Since I first need to understand how the sponsor environment works before we build our own analytics application, I will choose the forward engineering option. This means driven by requirements and therefore my terms will be business terms instead of application terms.

5. Operational or analytics?

This question ensures we choose the right type of BTM.

Did you choose operational or analytics for your initiative?

I need to analyze sponsor revenue, and therefore this will be for analytics and I will build a dimensional BTM. For your first model, make sure you choose dimensional as well.

6. Who is our audience?

That is, who is going to validate the model and who is going to use it going forward?

Who are the validators and users for your initiative?

My colleagues who help me organize the conferences will be the validators. They will be the ones who tell me if the model is correct or needs changes. The developer I hire to build the analytics application will be the user of the model. The developer can study my BTM and determine how best to build the application.

Step 2: Identify and define the terms

Now that we have direction, we can work with the business experts to identify the terms within the scope of the application and come up with an agreed-upon definition for each term. Identifying and defining the terms from a dimensional perspective involves defining the quantitative questions that the application will eventually answer.

What are the quantitative questions for your initiative?

Here are the quantitative questions for my Sponsor Initiative:

1. How much has each sponsor paid us by conference and country?
2. How much has each sponsor paid us by year, country, and level? Levels of sponsorship are Platinum, Gold, and Silver.
3. How much has each sponsor paid us by year?

On your dimensional BTM, if you sense any ambiguity in the terms used in the quantitative questions, go through a definition exercise. For example, if I felt the meaning of **Sponsor** lacked clarity I would work with the team to come up with one agreed upon definition for this term.

Step 3: Capture the relationships

For dimensional BTMs, we need to take the quantitative questions we identified in the prior step and then create a measure matrix. Recall that a measure matrix is a spreadsheet where the measures from the quantitative questions become columns and the dimensional levels from each quantitative question become rows.

For my Sponsor Initiative, let's plot the three questions on a measure matrix. The numbers in the measure matrix refer back to the previous three question numbers.

Sponsor Initiative measure matrix

	Sponsor Amount
Conference	1
Year	2,3
Country	1,2
Sponsor	1,2,3
Level	2

Complete a similar template for your initiative.

Step 4: Determine the most useful visual

I am a very big fan of the Axis Technique for a dimensional BTM, and so the following is my Sponsor Initiative BTM.

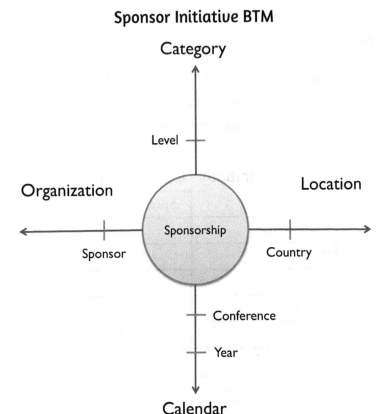

Sponsor Initiative BTM

Category

Level

Organization

Location

Sponsorship

Sponsor

Country

Conference

Year

Calendar

Create a BTM for your dimensional initiative.

Step 5: Review and confirm

Previously we identified the person or group responsible for validating the model. I will need to show my colleagues who help me organize the conferences the model and make sure it is correct. Often after reviewing the model, we can go back and make some changes and then show them the model again. This iterative cycle continues until the model is approved.

Takeaways

Do you feel more comfortable with building and using the relational and dimensional BTMs after reading the book and practicing in this chapter?

Just like anything new, the more you practice the better you get. You will find as you use this powerful communication tool that it becomes almost second nature to create these models whenever you sense the need for a Common Business Language.

Also, if you get hooked on BTMs and crave more on the data modeling side, expand your skillset into logical and physical data modeling. A good book to start with is my book, *Data Modeling Made Simple*. Shameless plug!

Good luck on your BTM adventures!

Index